APPALACHIAN TRAIL
Data Book
2006

APPALACHIAN TRAIL
Data Book
2006

TWENTY-EIGHTH EDITION

Daniel D. Chazin, *Editor*

APPALACHIAN TRAIL
CONSERVANCY

Harpers Ferry, West Virginia

Cover: Bog bridging north of Griffith Lake, Vermont
Photo © Laurie Potteiger

Twenty-eighth edition
First published in 1977

Printed on recycled paper

ISBN 1-889386-46-4

Contents

Notice to All Trail Users

The information in this publication is the result of the best effort of the publisher, using data available to it at the time of printing. Changes resulting from maintenance work and relocations are constantly occurring and, therefore, no published route can be regarded as precisely accurate at the time you read this notice.

Notices of pending relocations are indicated in current Appalachian Trail guidebooks.

Because maintenance of the Trail is conducted by volunteers and maintaining clubs listed in the appropriate guidebooks, questions about the exact route of the Trail should be addressed to the maintaining clubs or the Appalachian Trail Conservancy, P.O. Box 807, Harpers Ferry, WV 25425 (telephone: 304-535-6331; e-mail: info@appalachiantrail.org). On the Trail, please pay close attention to—and follow—the white blazes and any directional signs.

Planning and Safety

There are few things more rewarding than hiking the Appalachian Trail, whether you come to it as a novice looking to spend only a couple of hours outdoors or a Trail-tested veteran who has thru-hiked more than once.

Regardless of your skill, it is extremely important to plan your hike, especially in places where water is scarce. Purify water drawn from any source. Water purity cannot be guaranteed. The Appalachian Trail Conservancy and the various maintaining clubs attempt to locate good sources of water along the Trail but have no control over those sources and cannot, in any sense, be responsible for the quality of the water at any given time. You should ensure the safety of all water you use by treating it.

Certain risks are inherent in any Appalachian Trail hike. Each A.T. user must accept personal responsibility for his or her safety while on the Trail. The Appalachian Trail Conservancy and its member maintaining clubs cannot ensure the safety of any hiker on the Trail, and, when undertaking a hike on the Trail, each user thereby assumes the risk for any accident, illness, or injury that might occur on the Trail.

Enjoy your hike, but please take all appropriate precautions for your safety and well-being.

Hiker Awareness

Although the Appalachian Trail is safer than most places, you should be aware that problems do occur and a few crimes of violence have occurred during the past two decades. Hiker Awareness is one of your best lines of defense. Be aware of what you are doing, where you are, and to whom you are talking. Here are some suggestions:

- *Don't hike alone.* If you are by yourself and encounter a stranger who makes you feel uncomfortable, say you are with a group that is behind you. Be creative. If in doubt, move on.

- *Leave your hiking itinerary and timetable* with someone at home. Be sure he or she knows your Trail name, if you have one. Check in regularly, and establish a procedure to follow if you fail to check in. It helps to let ATC know your name and Trail name, in case a family member needs to reach you during an extended hike.

- *Be wary of strangers.* Be friendly, but cautious. Don't tell strangers your plans. Avoid people who act suspiciously, hostile, or intoxicated.

- *Don't camp near road crossings.*

- *Dress conservatively* to avoid unwanted attention.

- *Carrying firearms is strongly discouraged.* They are illegal on National Park Service lands and in most other areas without a permit, they could be turned against you, you face a high risk of an accidental shooting, and they are extra weight.

- *Eliminate opportunities for theft.* Don't bring jewelry. Hide your money. If you must leave your pack, hide it carefully, or leave it with someone trustworthy. Don't leave valuables or equipment (especially in sight) in vehicles parked at Trail-heads.

- *Use the Trail and shelter registers.* Sign in, leave a note, and report any suspicious activities. If someone needs to locate you, or if a serious crime has been committed along the Trail, the first place authorities will look is in the registers.

- *Report any crime or harassment* to the local law-enforcement authorities and ATC. Use the incident report form on page 87; cut out, fold, and mail it to ATC.

As the Trail becomes increasingly well known, the potential for problems could increase. Help to keep the Trail a safe place. Maintain your Hiker Awareness, help each other, and report all incidents. Be prudent and cautious without allowing common sense to slip into paranoia. Trust your gut.

Reporting Trail Emergencies

Check the guidebook, nearest shelter, or Trailhead facility for local emergency telephone numbers and the location of the nearest telephone. Leave the Trail at the nearest road crossing, and find a telephone. Know your location and the location of the incident as precisely as possible. Dial "911" or "0" (ask the operator to connect you with the nearest state police facility), and make your report. Ask the officer to notify the Appalachian Trail Conservancy at (304) 535-6331. Also, please fill out the form on page 87, and mail it to ATC from the next post office.

Leave No Trace

The Appalachian Trail Conservancy, in partnership with Leave No Trace, asks you to help take care of the Appalachian Trail and the wild country it passes through. Please do your part by following the seven Leave No Trace principles of low-impact use while in the backcountry:

1. Plan ahead and prepare.

2. Travel and camp on durable surfaces.

3. Dispose of waste properly.

4. Leave what you find.

5. Minimize campfire impacts.

6. Respect wildlife.

7. Be considerate of other visitors.

Useful Features of the *A.T. Data Book*

This publication provides a ready reference for hikers to the major features of the Appalachian Trail as it winds for almost 2,175 miles from Maine to Georgia. Many hikers find it indispensable to their journeys on the A.T. and save each year's edition as a record of their experiences and accomplishments.

The features listed here include shelters and campsites, road crossings, sources of water, elevations, principal mountain peaks and gaps, and other notable physical landmarks of America's first national scenic trail. Locations of areas where lodging, meals, groceries, and post offices are available also are listed, with distances and directions. Additionally, each section is marked with the Trail-maintaining club associated with that segment, and contact information for the clubs may be found on page 85.

The *Data Book* is intended to be useful in broad-scale planning of a trip of any length on the Trail, from home or while on the footpath itself.

The *Data Book* does not, however, include sufficient detail for careful, complete planning of a trip. Potential hikers are encouraged to purchase separately the *Appalachian Trail Guide* for the state(s) they plan to hike. The guidebooks contain detailed descriptions of Trail sections, facilities near the Trail, points of interest off the Trail, background on the history and natural features of the area, and other important information.

All guidebooks are sold with sets of maps for the state(s) described, another key to an enjoyable hike. Guidebooks, maps, and other ATC publications may be ordered by visiting the Ultimate A.T. Store at www.appalachiantrail.org, or by calling (304) 728-5143, or toll-free at (888) 287-8673. Membership in the Appalachian Trail Conservancy carries with it a discount on guidebooks and other publications.

The compilation of each edition of the *Data Book* begins with the latest *Appalachian Trail Guides*. The distances and descriptive information are updated to take into account relocations since the last edition.

This information is supplied to the Conservancy by its member clubs and volunteers who help ensure access to the Appalachian Trail experience for all. Each year more than 5,000 volunteers contribute around 190,000 hours of work to various projects along the Trail.

The data has been cross-checked by both volunteers and staff members. However, it is impossible to ensure absolute accuracy of the information, and changes may occur during the year of this edition. Trail-enhancing relocations that affect distances between major features are underway in many states. Also, severe weather conditions, fires, and other unpredictable developments might force temporary closings of a section.

Users of the Trail for any period of time should carefully follow the painted white blazes that mark the current route of the Trail.

Hikers finding errors or omissions in the *Data Book* are urged to report them, by e-mail to editor@appalachiantrail.org, or by mail to Data Book Editor, Appalachian Trail Conservancy, P.O. Box 807, Harpers Ferry, WV 25425. Confirmed changes will be included in the next edition.

The continued existence of the Appalachian Trail depends, in part, on proper use by those who walk on it. Particular care should be taken not to damage the footpath itself, natural features (geological or botanical) alongside it, or the property of others, through littering or other vandalism, improper fires, or use of vehicles. The needs of other users should always be considered, and special regulations must be followed in many areas. Please keep day-hiking groups to 25 people or fewer and overnight groups to no more than 10 people.

Although more than 99 percent of the Appalachian Trail now crosses public land, the remainder is on private property, thanks to the cooperation and good faith of the landowners. The Conservancy and its member clubs strongly urge all users of the Trail to respect those private lands and the owners' rights as if the lands were their own.

Public lands are, in a sense, the user's own—shared with all other users—so please proceed accordingly, taking care to obey any regulations imposed on use of the Trail in a particular section. For example, camping permits are required before entering Great Smoky Mountains National Park. On many other parts of the Trail, camping is permitted only in designated areas.

Again, please consult the guidebooks, and watch for special signs along the Trail.

And, enjoy your hike!

How to Use the *Data Book*

The Data Book is divided into eleven **chapters,** beginning with Maine (at Katahdin) and ending with Georgia (at Springer Mountain). With one exception, each chapter corresponds to a volume in the current series of *Appalachian Trail Guides* (see page 4 for ordering information). The section beginning on page 27 for example, matches the third volume in the guidebook series, which covers the Trail in Massachusetts–Connecticut. The exception is the Trail route through the Great Smokies of Tennessee and North Carolina, which is covered in both the Tennessee–North Carolina and North Carolina–Georgia guidebooks. It is included here only in Chapter Ten (Tennessee–North Carolina).

Trail-maintaining clubs are listed in the outside margins next to the section(s) of Trail that each club maintains. The beginning and ending points of each club's range are indicated by a small gray rectangle. Contact information for the clubs may be found on page 85.

Trail sections, as numbered and identified in the corresponding guide, are given in the columns to the left on each page, under the heading **GBS** (guidebook section). Except for the Shenandoah National Park chapter, sections are numbered consecutively, from north to south, within each state. (The sections in the Shenandoah National Park chapter are numbered independently of the remainder of Virginia, according to the latest edition of the guidebook for the park.)

In the right column, under the heading **Map**, the number of the map that covers the area is given. For more detail about a particular feature or section of the Trail, consult the relevant guidebook section or map.

Each section contains a list of **features** along or near the Trail:

Towns with post offices (P.O.) are printed in boldface and carry their ZIP Code in the listing. Towns without post offices are listed only if the Trail goes directly through them; "P.O." is omitted in those cases.

Greenwood Lake, N.Y., P.O. 10925

The **elevations** of selected points along the Trail follow the name of the feature. Those elevations are intended to represent the most significant points in terms of elevation gain and loss and provide the hiker with a general sense of the elevation change along each section of the hike. Of course, many ups and downs have not been referenced in this book, and the difficulty of the terrain may vary considerably. Hikers should use the elevations provided only as a general guide.

Rainbow Ledges (1,517')

In general, all **facilities** within five miles of the Trail by road are included, unless similar facilities are located closer to the footpath or a facility's inclusion would not significantly benefit the hiker. In some cases, where a particular facility is not available for a great distance, we have included facilities that are more than five miles from the Trail but still within 12 miles.

To the right of the list of features, **facilities**, if any, are noted with a one-letter code. The codes are explained on pages 8–9.

Low Gap   Cw

Except for shelters, campsites, and water sources located on the Trail itself—or within 0.1 mile of the footpath—the listing for a facility includes the distance and direction to it. So, if the symbols "C", "S", or "w" appear without direction and distance information in the listing, that campsite, shelter, or water source is on the Trail or within about 500 feet of it.

The number to the left of a feature is the **distance—in miles**—of the feature from the northern end of the part of the Trail covered in that particular chapter (read down). The number to the right of the features and facilities lists, correspondingly, is the feature's distance from the southern end of the part of the Trail covered by this chapter (read up). The starting point for the cumulative distance is given at the top of the column.

Miles from *Katahdin*		*Miles from* *Maine–N.H. Line*	
0.0	Katahdin (Baxter Peak) (5,268')		281.4
1.0	Thoreau Spring	w	280.4

Sometimes the Trail follows a road, ridge line, lake, creek, or other physical feature for some distance. In those cases, usually only one distance is listed. For roads, this is generally the point at which the Trail first reaches the road proceeding from north to south, or, in some cases, the point representing the end of the section. For ridge lines, this is the highest point. Again, for more complete information about a particular feature, please consult the guidebooks, maps, or both.

Abbreviations

C   **Campsites and campgrounds.** Unless otherwise indicated, water is available. For New Hampshire, the "C" code is also used to indicate those shelters at which tent camping is permitted.

E   **"East,"** used to designate direction to facilities that are to the right of the Trail when traveling north.

G   **Groceries, supplies.**

L   **Lodgings other than Trail shelters, campsites, and campgrounds:** for example, motels, hotels, cottages, and hostels. This code is also used for the Appalachian Mountain Club (AMC) huts in New Hampshire and camps (commercial cottages) in Maine.

m   **Miles.**

M   **Meals; restaurants.**

nw   **No potable water.** This is used in shelter and campsite listings only.

P.O.   **Post office.** Towns without post offices are listed only if the Trail goes directly through them; "P.O." is omitted in those cases.

R   **Road access.** Only roads open to the public and passable by ordinary automobiles are designated. Included are road crossings and locations where the Trail runs along a road or is adjacent to a road that provides access to the Trail. Where the road crossings are frequent (every two miles or less), lesser ones are omitted.

S   **Shelter.** A three-sided structure, with or without bunks or floors, intended as overnight housing for hikers (also known as lean-tos in many areas). Included in this category are unlocked cabins or lodges, found primarily in New Hampshire, Vermont, Pennsylvania, and Maryland. (See also "L".)

W   **"West,"** used to designate direction to facilities that are to the left of the Trail when traveling north.

w   **Water** (from springs, streams, etc.). In general, where available, water sources are listed about every three to four miles. Other water sources do exist, and not every water source is listed in the *Data Book*. ***Note:*** **All water should be purified before use.**

Appalachian Trail Distances

These sections and Trail points correspond to the beginnings and endings of chapters in this book and the eleven-volume series of Appalachian Trail Guides.

Length by Section

Maine	281.4
New Hampshire–Vermont	310.8
Massachusetts–Connecticut	141.8
New York–New Jersey	160.9
Pennsylvania	229.3
Maryland–West Virginia–Northern Virginia	94.9
Shenandoah National Park	107.1
Central Virginia	225.8
Southwest Virginia	163.1
Tennessee–North Carolina	296.2
North Carolina–Georgia	163.3

Cumulative Distances

Miles from Katahdin		Miles from Springer Mountain
0.0	Baxter Peak, Katahdin, Maine	2,175.6
281.4	Maine–New Hampshire Line	1,893.2
592.2	Vermont–Massachusetts Line	1,583.4
734.0	Connecticut–New York Line	1,441.6
894.9	New Jersey–Pennsylvania Line	1,279.7
1,124.2	Pennsylvania–Maryland Line	1,051.4
1,219.1	Front Royal, Virginia	956.5
1,326.2	Rockfish Gap, Virginia	849.4
1,552.0	New River, Virginia	622.6
1,715.1	Damascus, Virginia	459.5
2,011.3	Fontana Dam, North Carolina	163.3
2,175.6	Springer Mountain, Georgia	0.0

Maine

N to S	Features	Facilities	S to N
	Miles from Katahdin		*Miles from Maine–N.H. Line*
0.0	Katahdin (Baxter Peak) (5,268')		281.4
1.0	Thoreau Spring	w	280.4
4.0	Katahdin Stream Falls	w	277.4
5.2	Katahdin Stream Campground, Birches Campsite (1,070') (C,S,w on A.T.)	CSw	276.2
5.3	Pack Tote Road	R	276.1
7.6	Daicey Pond Campground (L,w 0.1m E)	RLw	273.8
8.8	Big Niagara Falls	w	272.6
11.0	Pine Point	w	270.4
14.0	Katahdin Stream	w	267.4
14.4	Abol Stream, Baxter Park Boundary		267.0
15.1	Abol Bridge over West Branch of Penobscot River; junction with International A.T. (588') (C,G,w on A.T.)	RCGw	266.3
18.6	Hurd Brook Lean-to (710')	Sw	262.8
21.1	Rainbow Ledges (1,517')		260.3
22.9	Rainbow Lake (east end)	w	258.5
26.3	Rainbow Spring Campsite	Cw	255.1
28.1	Rainbow Lake (west end) Side Trail	w	253.3
30.1	Rainbow Stream Lean-to (1,020')	Sw	251.3
32.5	Pollywog Stream (682')	w	248.9
33.9	Crescent Pond (west end)	w	247.5
36.3	Nesuntabunt Mountain (1,520')		245.1
38.2	Wadleigh Stream Lean-to	Sw	243.2

Maine Section 1

Maine Section 2

Maine A. T. Club

Maine Map 1

Maine

	Miles from Katahdin		Miles from Maine–N.H. Line		

N to S	Features	Facilities	S to N
40.8	Nahmakanta Lake (south end) (650')	Rw	240.6
44.0	Nahmakanta Stream Campsite	Cw	237.4
46.0	Logging Road (C,L,M 1m E)	RCLM	235.4
47.7	Pemadumcook Lake (southwest shore)	w	233.7
48.3	Potaywadjo Spring Lean-to (710')	Sw	233.1
50.1	Sand Beach, Lower Jo-Mary Lake	w	231.3
51.8	Antlers Campsite (500')	Cw	229.6
53.1	Mud Pond (outlet)	w	228.3
56.0	Jo-Mary Road (w on A.T.; C,G 6m E)	RCGw	225.4
59.7	Cooper Brook Falls Lean-to (880')	Sw	221.7
62.0	Crawford Pond (outlet)	w	219.4
62.9	Kokadjo–B Pond Road	R	218.5
64.3	Little Boardman Mountain (1,980')		217.1
65.6	Spring	w	215.8
65.9	Mountain View Pond (outlet)	w	215.5
67.5	East Branch of Pleasant River (ford)	w	213.9
67.8	East Branch Lean-to (1,225')	Sw	213.6
69.8	West Branch Ponds Road (L,M 4m W)	RLM	211.6
71.4	Logan Brook Lean-to (2,480')	Sw	210.0
72.8	White Cap Mountain (3,650')		208.6
73.9	White Brook Trail		207.5
74.5	Hay Mountain		206.9
76.1	West Peak		205.3
76.8	Sidney Tappan Campsite (2,425')	Cw	204.6
77.7	Gulf Hagas Mountain		203.7
78.6	Carl A. Newhall Lean-to (1,860')	Sw	202.8
82.1	Gulf Hagas Cut-off Trail	w	199.3

Maine A.T. Club
Maine Section 3

Maine Map 2

Maine

	Miles from Katahdin			Miles from Maine–N.H. Line	
	82.8	Gulf Hagas Trail	w	198.6	
	83.8	The Hermitage (695')			
		(C,w 0.7m E)	Cw	197.6	
	84.1	West Branch of Pleasant River (ford)	w	197.3	
	84.6	Logging Road	R	196.8	
	85.8	East Chairback Pond Side Trail (1,630')			
		(w 0.2m W)	w	195.6	
	88.0	Chairback Mountain (2,180')		193.4	
	88.5	Chairback Gap Lean-to (1,930')	Sw	192.9	
	88.9	Columbus Mountain (2,325')		192.5	
	90.2	West Chairback Pond Side Trail (1,770')	w	191.2	
	90.8	Third Mountain, Monument Cliff (1,920')		190.6	
	93.3	Fourth Mountain (2,380')		188.1	
	95.4	Cloud Pond Lean-to Side Trail			
		(S,w 0.3m E)	Sw	186.0	
	96.3	Barren Mountain (2,660')		185.1	
	99.4	Long Pond Stream Lean-to (940')	Sw	182.0	
	100.2	Long Pond Stream (ford) (620')	w	181.2	
	104.1	Wilson Valley Lean-to (1,045')	Sw	177.3	
	104.5	Canadian Pacific Railroad		176.9	
	104.8	Big Wilson Stream (ford) (600')	w	176.6	
	107.7	Little Wilson Stream	w	173.7	
	107.9	Little Wilson Falls		173.5	
	110.7	North Pond (outlet)	w	170.7	
	111.5	Leeman Brook Lean-to (1,060')	Sw	169.9	
	112.6	Lily Pond	w	168.8	
	113.3	Bell Pond	w	168.1	
	114.4	Spectacle Pond (outlet)	w	167.0	
	114.5	Maine 15 (1,215')	R	166.9	

Maine 3 · *Maine Section 4* · *Map 2* · *Maine Map 3* · *Maine A.T. Club*

Maine

Miles from Katahdin

Miles from Maine–N.H. Line

	N to S	Features	Facilities	S to N	
	117.8	**Monson, Maine, P.O. 04464** (900') (P.O.,C,G,L,M 2m E)	CGLM	163.6	
	120.8	Shirley–Blanchard Road	R	160.6	
	121.2	East Branch of Piscataquis River (ford)	w	160.2	
	123.5	Horseshoe Canyon Lean-to (870')	Sw	157.9	
	126.6	West Branch of Piscataquis River (ford)	w	154.8	
	130.3	Bald Mountain Pond (outlet)	w	151.1	
	132.4	Moxie Bald Lean-to (1,220')	Sw	149.0	
	134.5	Moxie Bald Mountain (2,629')		146.9	
	136.5	Bald Mountain Brook Lean-to (1,300')	Sw	144.9	
	139.3	Moxie Pond (south end) (970')	Rw	142.1	
	144.2	Pleasant Pond Mountain (2,470')		137.2	
	145.5	Pleasant Pond Lean-to (1,320')	Sw	135.9	
	145.9	Boise-Cascade Logging Road	R	135.5	
	148.5	Holly Brook	w	132.9	
	151.2	U.S. 201; **Caratunk, Maine, P.O. 04925** (P.O. 0.3m E; C,G,L 1.0m W)	RCGL	130.2	
	151.5	Kennebec River (490')	w	129.9	
	154.8	Trail to Harrison's Pierce Pond Camps (L,M 0.3m E; w 0.1m E)	RLMw	126.6	
	155.2	Pierce Pond Lean-to (1,160')	Sw	126.2	
	158.7	North Branch of Carrying Place Stream	w	122.7	
	159.4	Logging Road	R	122.0	
	161.1	East Carry Pond (north end)	w	120.3	
	162.6	Sandy Stream, Middle Carry Pond (inlet)	w	118.8	
	164.5	West Carry Pond (east side)	w	116.9	
	165.2	West Carry Pond Lean-to (1,340')	Sw	116.2	
	165.9	West Carry Pond (west side)	w	115.5	
	167.0	Roundtop Mountain (1,760')		114.4	

Maine A.T. Club

Maine Section 5

Maine Section 6

Maine Map 4

Maine Map 5

Maine

	Miles from Katahdin			*Miles from Maine–N.H. Line*	
	168.7	Long Falls Dam Road (1,225')	R	112.7	
	171.0	Bog Brook Road, Flagstaff Lake (inlet)	Rw	110.4	
	171.1	East Flagstaff Road	R	110.3	
	172.5	Little Bigelow Lean-to (1,760')	Sw	108.9	
	174.2	Little Bigelow Mountain (east end) (3,010')		107.2	
	177.4	Safford Notch Campsite (2,230') (C,w 0.3m E)	Cw	104.0	
	177.5	Safford Brook Trail		103.9	
	179.4	Bigelow Mountain (Avery Peak) (4,090')		102.0	
	179.8	Avery Memorial Campsite, Bigelow Col, Fire Warden's Trail	Cw	101.6	
	180.1	Bigelow Mountain (West Peak) (4,145')		101.3	
	182.2	South Horn		99.2	
	182.7	Horns Pond Lean-tos (3,160')	CSw	98.7	
	182.9	Horns Pond Trail		98.5	
	184.6	Bigelow Range Trail, Cranberry Pond (w 0.2m W)	w	96.8	
	185.9	Cranberry Stream Campsite (1,350')	Cw	95.5	
	186.8	Stratton Brook (1,230')	w	94.6	
	187.0	Stratton Brook Pond Road	R	94.4	
	187.8	Maine 27; **Stratton, Maine, P.O. 04982** (P.O.,G,L,M 5m W)	RGLM	93.6	
	193.0	North Crocker Mountain (4,228')		88.4	
	194.0	South Crocker Mountain (4,040')		87.4	
	195.1	Crocker Cirque Campsite Side Trail (2,710') (w on A.T.; C 0.2m E)	Cw	86.3	
	196.1	Caribou Valley Road (2,220')	R	85.3	
	196.2	South Branch Carrabassett River (ford)	w	85.2	
	198.4	Sugarloaf Mountain Trail		83.0	
	200.5	Spaulding Mountain (4,000')		80.9	

Maine Section 7

Maine Section 8

Maine Map 5

Maine Map 6

Maine A.T. Club

Maine

GBS	N to S	Features	Facilities (see page 8 for codes)	S to N	Map
		Miles from Katahdin		*Miles from Maine–N.H. Line*	
	201.3	Spaulding Mountain Lean-to (3,140')	Sw	80.1	
	202.4	Mt. Abraham Trail		79.0	
	203.5	Lone Mountain (3,260')		77.9	
	206.6	Orbeton Stream (ford) (1,550')	w	74.8	
	209.3	Poplar Ridge Lean-to (2,960')	Sw	72.1	
	210.3	Stream	w	71.1	
	210.7	Saddleback Junior (3,655')		70.7	
	212.7	The Horn (4,040')		68.7	
	214.3	Saddleback Mountain (4,120')		67.1	
	216.3	Eddy Pond	w	65.1	
	218.2	Piazza Rock Lean-to (2,065')	Sw	63.2	
	219.9	Sandy River (1,595')	w	61.5	
	220.0	Maine 4; **Rangeley, Maine, P.O. 04970** (P.O.,C,G,L,M 9m W)	RCGLM	61.4	
	222.1	South Pond (2,174')	w	59.3	
	224.8	Little Swift River Pond Campsite (2,460')	Cw	56.6	
	229.4	Sabbath Day Pond Lean-to	Sw	52.0	
	229.7	Long Pond (2,330')	w	51.7	
	231.5	Moxie Pond	w	49.9	
	233.1	Maine 17; **Oquossoc, Maine, P.O. 04964** (P.O.,G,L,M 11m W)	RGLM	48.3	
	233.9	Bemis Stream (ford) (1,495')	w	47.5	
	237.7	Bemis Mountain Lean-to (2,800')	Sw	43.7	
	239.4	Bemis Range (West Peak) (3,580')		42.0	
	240.4	Bemis Stream Trail		41.0	
	243.6	Old Blue Mountain (3,600')		37.8	
	246.4	South Arm Road, Black Brook (ford) (1,410') (w on A.T.; C,G 4.5m W)	RCGw	35.0	
	248.2	Moody Mountain (2,440)		33.2	

Maine A.T. Club

Maine Section 8 · Maine Section 9 · Maine 10 · Maine 11

Maine Map 6 · Maine Map 7

Maine

GBS	N to S	Features	Facilities (see page 8 for codes)	S to N	Map
	Miles from Katahdin			*Miles from Maine–N.H. Line*	
Maine 11	249.1	Sawyer Notch, Sawyer Brook (ford) (1,095')	w	32.3	Maine Map 7
	250.5	Hall Mountain Lean-to (2,650')	Sw	30.9	
	251.8	Wyman Mountain (2,920')		29.6	
	254.7	Surplus Pond (outlet)	w	26.7	
Maine Section 12	256.5	East B Hill Road (1,485'); **Andover, Maine, P.O. 04216** (P.O.,C,G,L,M 8m E)	RCGLM	24.9	
	257.3	Dunn Notch and Falls	w	24.1	
	261.0	Frye Notch Lean-to (2,280')	Sw	20.4	
	262.8	Baldpate Mountain (East Peak), Grafton Loop Trail (3,810')		18.6	
	263.7	Baldpate Mountain (West Peak) (3,662')		17.7	
	264.5	Baldpate Lean-to (2,660')	Sw	16.9	
Maine Section 13	266.8	Grafton Notch, Maine 26 (1,495')	R	14.6	
	267.9	Brook	w	13.5	
	270.3	Old Speck Trail (3,985')		11.1	
	271.4	Speck Pond Campsite, Speck Pond Trail	CSw	10.0	
	272.3	Mahoosuc Arm (3,770')		9.1	
	273.9	Mahoosuc Notch (east end) (2,150')	w	7.5	
	275.0	Mahoosuc Notch (west end), Mahoosuc Notch Trail	w	6.4	
	276.0	Fulling Mill Mountain (South Peak) (3,395')	5.4		
	276.5	Full Goose Shelter and Campsite	CSw	4.9	
	277.5	Goose Eye Mountain (North Peak)		3.9	
	278.7	Goose Eye Mountain (East Peak) (3,790')		2.7	
	280.5	Mt. Carlo (3,565')		0.9	
	280.9	Carlo Col Trail, Carlo Col Shelter and Campsite (C,S,w 0.3m W)	CSw	0.5	
	281.4	Maine–New Hampshire Line (2,972')		0.0	

Maine Appalachian Trail Club

Appalachian Mountain Club

GBS	N to S	Features	Facilities (see page 8 for codes)	S to N	Map

Miles from Maine–N.H. Line

Miles from Vt.–Mass. Line

	N to S	Features	Facilities	S to N	
	0.0	Maine–New Hampshire Line (2,972')		310.8	
	1.9	Mt. Success (3,565')		308.9	
	4.7	Gentian Pond Campsite (2,166')	CSw	306.1	
	5.4	Moss Pond	w	305.4	
	6.9	Dream Lake	w	303.9	
	9.6	Trident Col Tentsite (2,000')	Cw	301.2	
	10.7	Cascade Mountain (2,631')		300.1	
	15.0	Brook	w	295.8	
	16.2	Androscoggin River (750')	R	294.6	
	16.5	U.S. 2; **Gorham, N.H., P.O. 03581** (w on A.T.; P.O.,G,L,M 3.6m W; C,G 1m E; C,L,M 2m W)	RCGLMw	294.3	
	18.4	Rattle River Shelter	Sw	292.4	
	22.4	Mt. Moriah (4,049')		288.4	
	24.5	Imp Campsite (3,250')	CSw	286.3	
	27.0	Middle Carter Mountain (4,600')		283.8	
	29.1	Zeta Pass (3,990')		281.7	
	30.5	Carter Dome (4,832')		280.3	
	31.0	Spring	w	279.8	
	31.7	Carter Notch, Carter Notch Hut (3,350') (L,w 0.1m E)	Lw	279.1	
	32.6	Wildcat Mountain, Peak A (4,380')		278.2	
	34.6	Wildcat Mountain, Peak D		276.2	
	37.6	Pinkham Notch, N.H. 16, Pinkham Notch Camp (2,050') (L,M,w on A.T.)	RLMw	273.2	
	39.5	Lowe's Bald Spot (2,860')		271.3	
	41.6	West Branch, Peabody River (2,300')	w	269.2	
	42.4	Osgood Tentsite	Cw	268.4	
	44.9	Mt. Madison (5,363')		265.9	

Left margin: *Appalachian Mountain Club* — N.H. Section 1 / N.H. Section 2 / N.H. Section 3

Right margin: N.H.–Vt. Map 1 / N.H.–Vt. Map 2

New Hampshire–Vermont

	Miles from Maine–N.H. Line			*Miles from Vt.–Mass. Line*	
	45.4	Madison Springs Hut, Valley Way Tentsite (C,w 0.6m W; L,M,w on A.T.)	CLMw	265.4	
	46.3	Thunderstorm Junction, Spur Trail to Crag Camp Cabin, Lowe's Path to Mt. Adams & Gray Knob Cabin (C,S,w 1.1m W, 1.2m W)	CSw	264.5	
	46.9	Israel Ridge Path to The Perch Shelter (C,S,w 0.9m W)	CSw	263.9	
	47.6	Edmands Col (5,000')		263.2	
	51.0	**Mt. Washington, N.H., P.O. 03589** (6,288') (P.O.,M on A.T.)	RM	259.8	
	52.4	Lakes of the Clouds Hut (5,000') (L,M,w on A.T.)	LMw	258.4	
	53.9	Mt. Franklin		256.6	
	54.2	Spring	w	256.6	
	55.5	Spring	w	255.3	
	56.4	Mt. Pierce (Mt. Clinton)		254.4	
	57.2	Mizpah Spring Hut, Nauman Tentsite (3,800') (C,L,M,w on A.T.)	CLMw	253.6	
	58.9	Mt. Jackson		251.9	
	60.3	Mt. Webster (3,910')		250.5	
	63.5	Saco River		247.3	
	63.6	Crawford Notch, U.S. 302, Dry River Campground (1,277') (C 1.8m E; M 1m W)	RCM	247.2	
	66.5	Ethan Pond Campsite (2,950')	CSw	244.3	
	71.3	Zealand Falls Hut (2,450') (L,M,w on A.T.)	LMw	239.5	

N.H. Section 3 / *N.H. Section 4*

N.H.–Vt. Map 2 / *Appalachian Mountain Club* / *Map 3*

New Hampshire–Vermont

	Miles from Maine–N.H. Line		*Miles from Vt.–Mass. Line*	

N.H. Section 4	72.5	Zeacliff		238.3
	75.5	Mt. Guyot, Guyot Campsite (4,560') (C,S,w 0.7m E)	CSw	235.3
	77.5	South Twin Mountain, North Twin Spur (4,902')		233.3
	78.3	Galehead Hut (L,M,w on A.T.)	LMw	232.5
	81.0	Garfield Ridge Campsite (3,500')	CSw	229.8
	81.4	Mt. Garfield (4,488')		229.4
	84.9	Mt. Lafayette, Greenleaf Hut (5,249') (L,M 1.1m W; w 0.2m W)	LMw	225.9
	85.9	Mt. Lincoln		224.9
	86.6	Little Haystack Mountain		224.2
	88.7	Liberty Spring Tentsite (3,800')	Cw	222.1
	91.3	Franconia Notch, U.S. 3, Lafayette Place Campground (1,450'); **North Woodstock, N.H., P.O. 03262** (P.O.,G,L,M 5.8m E; G,L,M 2.2m E; C 2.1m W; L 1.6m E)	RCGLM	219.5
N.H. Section 5	94.2	Lonesome Lake Hut (2,760') (L,M,w on A.T.)	LMw	216.6
	96.1	Kinsman Pond Campsite	CSw	214.7
	96.7	North Kinsman Mountain		214.1
	97.6	South Kinsman Mountain (4,358')		213.2
	100.1	Eliza Brook Shelter (2,500')	Sw	210.7
	103.0	Mt. Wolf (East Peak) (3,478')		207.8
	107.6	Kinsman Notch, N.H. 112 (1,812')	R	203.2
N.H. 6	109.2	Beaver Brook Shelter (3,650')	Sw	201.6
	111.4	Mt. Moosilauke (4,802')		199.4
	116.0	Jeffers Brook Shelter (1,350')	Sw	194.8

Appalachian Mountain Club

DOC

N.H.–Vt. Map 3

New Hampshire–Vermont

GBS	N to S	Features	Facilities (see page 8 for codes)	S to N	Map
	Miles from Maine–N.H. Line			*Miles from Vt.–Mass. Line*	
N.H. Section 7	117.1	N.H. 25 (1,140'); **Glencliff, N.H., P.O. 03238** (P.O.,L 0.5m E)	RL	193.7	
	119.6	Mt. Mist (2,200')		191.2	
	122.1	N.H. 25C (1,500'); **Warren, N.H., P.O. 03279** (w on A.T.; P.O.,G,M 4m E)	RGMw	188.7	
	124.5	Ore Hill Shelter	CSw	186.3	
	125.1	Cape Moonshine Road	R	185.7	
N.H. Section 8	126.9	N.H. 25A (900'); **Wentworth, N.H., P.O. 03282** (P.O.,G 4.8m E)	RG	183.9	N.H.–Vt. Map 4
	130.2	Side trail to Mt. Cube (North Summit) (2,911')		180.6	
	131.8	Hexacuba Shelter (w on A.T.; S 0.3m E)	Sw	179.0	
	133.2	South Jacob's Brook (1,450')	w	177.6	
	137.1	Firewarden's Cabin (3,240')	Sw	173.7	
	137.2	Smarts Mountain Tentsite	Cw	173.6	
	140.9	Lyme–Dorchester Road	Rw	169.9	
	142.9	Dartmouth Skiway (880'); **Lyme, N.H., P.O. 03768** (P.O.,G,L,M 3.2m W)	RGLM	167.9	
N.H. Section 9	143.8	Trapper John Shelter (S,w 0.2m W)	Sw	167.0	
	144.3	Holts Ledge (2,100')		166.5	
	146.3	Goose Pond Road (920')	R	164.5	
	147.6	South Fork Hewes Brook	w	163.2	
	149.5	Moose Mountain Shelter	Sw	161.3	
	150.3	Moose Mountain (South Peak) (2,250')		160.5	

Dartmouth Outing Club (DOC)

New Hampshire–Vermont

GBS	N to S	Features	Facilities (see page 8 for codes)	S to N	Map
	Miles from Maine–N.H. Line			*Miles from Vt.–Mass. Line*	
	151.9	Mink Brook	w	158.9	
	152.1	Three Mile Road	R	158.7	
	154.6	Etna–Hanover Center Road (880'); **Etna, N.H., P.O. 03750** (P.O. 1.2m E)	R	156.2	
	156.0	Trescott Road	R	154.8	
	158.5	Ledyard Spring (w 0.2m W)	w	152.3	
	159.0	Velvet Rocks Shelter (S 0.2m W)	S	151.8	
	159.8	N.H. 120	R	151.0	
	160.5	Dartmouth College; **Hanover, N.H., P.O. 03755** (P.O.,G,L,M on A.T.)	RGLM	150.3	
	161.0	New Hampshire–Vermont Line, Connecticut River (400')	R	149.8	
	162.0	**Norwich, Vt., P.O. 05055** (P.O.,G,L,M 0.3m W)	RGLM	148.8	
	166.3	Happy Hill Shelter (1,400')	Sw	144.5	
	168.9	Podunk Brook, Podunk Road	Rw	141.9	
	169.7	Tigertown Road, Podunk Road	R	141.1	
	170.3	Vt. 14, White River (400'); **West Hartford, Vt., P.O. 05084** (G,M,w on A.T.; P.O. 0.3m E)	RGMw	140.5	
	173.6	Joe Ranger Road	R	137.2	
	175.1	Thistle Hill Shelter	Sw	135.7	
	175.4	Thistle Hill (1,950')		135.4	
	177.4	Cloudland Road	R	133.4	
	179.2	South Pomfret–Pomfret Road	Rw	131.6	

Dartmouth Outing Club (DOC)

N.H. Section 9 · Vt. Section 1 · Vt. Section 2

N.H.–Vt. Map 4 · N.H.–Vt. Map 5

New Hampshire–Vermont

GBS	N to S	Features	Facilities (see page 8 for codes)	S to N	Map

	N to S	Features	Facilities	S to N	
Vt. 2	181.4	Woodstock Stage (Barnard Brook) Road (770'); **South Pomfret, Vt., P.O. 05067** (w on A.T.; P.O.,G 1m E)	RGw	129.4	
	182.9	Vt. 12 (882'); **Woodstock, Vt., P.O. 05091** (P.O.,G,L,M 4.4m E)	RGLM	127.9	
Vt. Section 3	186.7	Wintturi Shelter (1,900') (S,w 0.2m W)	Sw	124.1	
	189.1	Side trail to The Lookout		121.7	
	191.9	Chateauguay Road	R	118.9	
	196.6	Stony Brook Shelter (1,760')	Sw	114.2	
	200.9	River Road (1,214')	R	109.9	
	202.3	Thundering Brook Road, Kent Pond (L,M,w on A.T.)	RLMw	108.5	
	203.3	Vt. 100, Gifford Woods State Park	RCSw	107.5	
	204.7	Sherburne Pass Trail (2,440')		106.1	
	205.6	Junction with Long Trail, Tucker-Johnson Shelter (S,w 0.4m W)	Sw	105.2	
Vt. Section 4	206.6	U.S. 4 (1,880'); **Killington, Vt., P.O. 05751** (P.O. 2.2m E; L,M 1m E; G 2.6m E)	RGLM	104.2	
	208.5	Churchill Scott Shelter	Sw	102.3	
	210.4	Sherburne Pass Trail, Pico Camp (3,400') (S,w 0.5m E)	Sw	100.4	
	212.9	Cooper Lodge, Killington Peak Trail (3,850') (S,w on A.T.; M 0.2m E)	MSw	97.9	
	217.2	Governor Clement Shelter (1,850')	Sw	93.6	

Green Mountain Club *DOC*

N.H.–Vt. Map 5

N.H.–Vt. Map 6

New Hampshire–Vermont

GBS	N to S	Features	Facilities (see page 8 for codes)	S to N	Map

Miles from Maine–N.H. Line

Miles from Vt.–Mass. Line

<table>
<tr><td></td><td>218.6</td><td>Upper Cold River Road</td><td>Rw</td><td>92.2</td><td></td></tr>
<tr><td></td><td>219.3</td><td>Gould Brook (1,480')</td><td>w</td><td>91.5</td><td></td></tr>
<tr><td></td><td>220.1</td><td>Cold River Road (Lower Road)</td><td>R</td><td>90.7</td><td></td></tr>
<tr><td></td><td>222.1</td><td>Lottery Road</td><td>R</td><td>88.7</td><td></td></tr>
<tr><td></td><td>222.5</td><td>Beacon Hill</td><td></td><td>88.3</td><td></td></tr>
<tr><td></td><td>223.0</td><td>Clarendon Shelter</td><td>Sw</td><td>87.8</td><td></td></tr>
<tr><td></td><td>224.0</td><td>Vt. 103 (860'); North Clarendon, Vt., P.O. 05759 (P.O.,G,L 4.2m W; M 0.5m W; G 1m W; L 3m W)</td><td>RGLM</td><td>86.8</td><td></td></tr>
<tr><td></td><td>224.1</td><td>Clarendon Gorge, Mill River Bridge</td><td>w</td><td>86.7</td><td></td></tr>
<tr><td></td><td>226.7</td><td>Minerva Hinchey Shelter (1,530')</td><td>Sw</td><td>84.1</td><td></td></tr>
<tr><td></td><td>230.3</td><td>Vt. 140 (1,160'); Wallingford, Vt., P.O. 05773 (w on A.T.; P.O.,G,L,M 2.8m W; G 3.7m E)</td><td>RGLMw</td><td>80.5</td><td></td></tr>
<tr><td></td><td>230.4</td><td>Sugar Hill Road</td><td>R</td><td>80.4</td><td></td></tr>
<tr><td></td><td>231.8</td><td>Greenwall Shelter (S,w 0.2m E)</td><td>Sw</td><td>79.0</td><td></td></tr>
<tr><td></td><td>232.3</td><td>Trail to White Rocks Cliff (2,400')</td><td></td><td>78.5</td><td></td></tr>
<tr><td></td><td>236.2</td><td>Little Rock Pond Shelter</td><td>S</td><td>74.6</td><td></td></tr>
<tr><td></td><td>236.3</td><td>Green Mountain Trail to Homer Stone Brook Trail (G 2.3m W)</td><td>G</td><td>74.5</td><td></td></tr>
<tr><td></td><td>236.5</td><td>Spring</td><td>w</td><td>74.3</td><td></td></tr>
<tr><td></td><td>236.6</td><td>Little Rock Pond Tenting Area</td><td>Cw</td><td>74.2</td><td></td></tr>
<tr><td></td><td>236.9</td><td>Lula Tye Shelter</td><td>S</td><td>73.9</td><td></td></tr>
<tr><td></td><td>238.6</td><td>Danby–Landgrove Road (USFS 10), Black Branch (1,500'); Danby, Vt., P.O. 05739 (P.O.,G,L,M 3.5m W)</td><td>RGLM</td><td>72.2</td><td></td></tr>
</table>

Green Mountain Club

Vt. Section 4

Vt. Section 5

N.H.–Vt. Map 6

New Hampshire–Vermont

	Miles from Maine–N.H. Line			Miles from Vt.–Mass. Line
	239.9	Big Branch Shelter	Sw	70.9
	240.1	Old Job Trail to Old Job Shelter		
		(S,w 1m E)	Sw	70.7
	241.6	Lost Pond Shelter	Sw	69.2
	243.6	Baker Peak (2,850')		67.2
	245.6	Griffith Lake (north end)	w	65.2
	245.8	Griffith Lake Tenting Area	Cw	65.0
	246.3	Peru Peak Shelter	Sw	64.5
	247.6	Peru Peak (3,429')		63.2
	249.3	Styles Peak		61.5
	250.9	Mad Tom Notch, USFS 21 (2,446');		
		Peru, Vt., P.O. 05152		
		(P.O.,G 4.3m E; C 2.5m E)	RCGw	59.9
	253.4	Bromley Mountain (3,260')		57.4
	254.4	Bromley Shelter	Sw	56.4
	256.4	Vt. 11 & 30 (1,800');		
		Manchester Center, Vt., P.O. 05255		
		(P.O.,G,L,M 5.5m W;		
		G 2.5m E; L,M 0.6m E)	RGLM	54.4
	258.8	Spruce Peak		52.0
	259.2	Spruce Peak Shelter	Sw	51.6
	261.3	Old Rootville Road, Prospect Rock	R	49.5
	262.2	Branch Pond Trail to		
		William B. Douglas Shelter		
		(S,w 0.5m W)	Sw	48.6
	265.0	Winhall River	w	45.8
	266.9	Stratton Pond, North Shore Trail		
		to North Shore Tenting Area (2,555')		
		(w on A.T.; C,w 0.5m W)	Cw	43.9

Vt. Section 6
Vt. Section 7

N.H.–Vt. Map 7
Green Mountain Club

New Hampshire–Vermont

	Miles from Maine–N.H. Line			Miles from Vt.–Mass. Line	
	267.0	Stratton Pond Trail, Stratton Pond Shelter	Sw	43.8	
	270.1	Stratton Mountain (3,936')			
		(G,M 1.7m E)	GM	40.7	
	273.9	Stratton–Arlington Road			
		(Kelley Stand Road) (2,330')	Rw	36.9	
	277.5	Story Spring Shelter	Sw	33.3	
	278.4	South Alder Brook	w	32.4	
	282.1	Caughnawaga and Kid Gore Shelters	Sw	28.7	
	286.1	Glastenbury Mountain (3,748')		24.7	
	286.4	Goddard Shelter	Sw	24.4	
	288.9	Glastenbury Lookout		21.9	
	290.7	Little Pond Lookout (3,060')		20.1	
	293.3	Hell Hollow Brook	w	17.5	
	294.9	Melville Nauheim Shelter	Sw	15.9	
	296.5	City Stream, Vt. 9 (1,360');			
		Bennington, Vt., P.O. 05201			
		(P.O.,G,L,M 5.1m W;			
		L 2.4m W, 2.7m E; G 3.9m W)	RGLMw	14.3	
	298.3	Harmon Hill (2,325')		12.5	
	300.8	Congdon Shelter	Sw	10.0	
	305.0	Roaring Branch	w	5.8	
	307.7	County Road	R	3.1	
	308.0	Seth Warner Shelter and Primitive Camping Area			
		(C,S,w 0.2m W)	CSw	2.8	
	310.4	Brook	w	0.4	
	310.8	Vermont–Massachusetts Line, southern end of Long Trail (2,330')		0.0	

Vt. 7 · Vt. Section 8 · Vt. Section 9 · Green Mountain Club

Map 7 · N.H.–Vt. Map 8

Massachusetts–Connecticut

GBS	N to S	Features	Facilities (see page 8 for codes)	S to N	Map

Miles from Vt.–Mass. Line

Miles from Conn.–N.Y. Line

	N to S	Features	Facilities	S to N	
Mass. 1	0.0	Vermont–Massachusetts Line, southern end of Long Trail (2,330')		141.8	AMC Berkshire Chapter
	0.8	Eph's Lookout		141.0	
	1.3	Pine Cobble Trail		140.5	
	2.3	Sherman Brook Campsite	Cw	139.5	
	4.1	Mass. 2 (650'); **North Adams, Mass., P.O. 01247; Williamstown, Mass., P.O. 01267** (P.O.,G,L,M 2.5m E, 2.6m W; G,M 0.7m E; G,L,M 0.5m W)	RGLM	137.7	
Mass. Section 2	5.0	Pattison Road	Rw	136.8	
	7.1	Wilbur Clearing Lean-to (2,300') (C,S,w 0.3m W)	CSw	134.7	Mass.–Conn. Map 1
	7.2	Notch Road	Rw	134.6	
	10.4	Mt. Greylock, Summit Road, Bascom Lodge (3,491') (L,M,w on A.T.)	RLMw	131.4	
	10.9	Notch Road, Rockwell Road	R	130.9	
	13.1	Jones Nose Trail		128.7	
	13.7	Mark Noepel Lean-to (2,800') (C,S,w 0.2m E)	CSw	128.1	
	14.6	Old Adams Road	R	127.2	
	17.3	Outlook Avenue	R	124.5	
Mass. Section 3	18.1	Mass. 8 (1,000'); **Cheshire, Mass., P.O. 01225** (P.O. on A.T.; L 0.2m W; G,M 0.5m W)	RGLM	123.7	
	18.7	Hoosic River, Church Street	R	123.1	
	19.8	The Cobbles		122.0	
	22.3	Gore Pond (2,050')		119.5	

Massachusetts–Connecticut

Miles from Vt.–Mass. Line   *Miles from Conn.–N.Y. Line*

	N to S	Features	Facilities	S to N	
	22.7	Crystal Mountain Campsite (C,w 0.2m E)	Cw	119.1	
	26.4	Gulf Road	R	115.4	
	27.4	Mass. 8, Mass. 9 (1,200'); **Dalton, Mass., P.O. 01226** (M on A.T.; P.O.,G,L,M 0.3m W)	RGLM	114.4	
	28.0	CSX Railroad		113.8	
	30.1	Grange Hall Road	R	111.7	
	30.4	Kay Wood Lean-to (S,w 0.2m E)	Sw	111.4	
	33.1	Warner Mountain (2,050')		108.7	
	33.8	Blotz Road	R	108.0	
	35.0	Stream	w	106.8	
	37.0	Pittsfield Road (Washington Mountain Road); **Becket, Mass., P.O. 01223** (P.O.,G,L 5m E; M 1.8m E)	RGLM	104.8	
	38.5	West Branch Road	R	103.3	
	39.2	October Mountain Lean-to (1,950')	CSw	102.6	
	40.8	Bald Top		101.0	
	41.0	County Road	R	100.8	
	43.3	Finerty Pond	w	98.5	
	45.1	Becket Mountain (2,180')		96.7	
	45.6	Tyne Road	R	96.2	
	46.4	U.S. 20 (1,400'); **Lee, Mass., P.O. 01238** (P.O.,G,L,M 5m W; L 0.2m E; M 0.3m W)	RGLM	95.4	
	46.7	Greenwater Brook	w	95.1	
	46.8	Massachusetts Turnpike		95.0	
	48.0	Upper Goose Pond Cabin (C,S,w 0.5m W)	CSw	93.8	

Left margin sections: AMC Berkshire Chapter — Mass. 3, Mass. Section 4, Mass. Section 5, Mass. Section 6

Right margin maps: Map 1, Mass.–Conn. Map 2, Map 3

Massachusetts–Connecticut

	N to S	Features	Facilities (see page 8 for codes)	S to N	Map
	Miles from Vt.–Mass. Line			*Miles from Conn.–N.Y. Line*	
Mass. 6	48.8	Upper Goose Pond		93.0	
	50.7	Goose Pond Road	R	91.1	
	53.1	Webster Road (1,800')	Rw	88.7	
	55.0	Tyringham Main Road (930'); **Tyringham, Mass., P.O. 01264** (P.O. 0.9m W)	R	86.8	
Mass. Section 7	56.1	Jerusalem Road	Rw	85.7	
	57.9	Shaker Campsite	C	83.9	
	58.2	Fernside Road	Rw	83.6	
	61.4	Beartown Mountain Road	Rw	80.4	
	62.0	Mt. Wilcox North Lean-to (2,100') (S,w 0.3m E)	Sw	79.8	
	63.8	Mt. Wilcox South Lean-to	Sw	78.0	
	64.5	The Ledges		77.3	
	65.1	Benedict Pond (C,w 0.5m w)	RCw	76.7	
	65.9	Blue Hill Road (Stony Brook Road)	R	75.9	
	67.1	Mass. 23 (1,000'); **Great Barrington, Mass., P.O. 01230** (P.O.,G,L,M 4m W; L 0.1m E)	RGLM	74.7	
Mass. Section 8	68.0	Lake Buel Road (L,M 2.5m W)	RLM	73.8	
	69.1	Ice Gulch, Tom Leonard Lean-to (S on A.T.; w 0.2m E)	Sw	72.7	
	71.2	East Mountain (1,800')	w	70.6	
	72.6	Homes Road	R	69.2	
	74.6	Housatonic River	R	67.2	
	75.5	U.S. 7; **Sheffield, Mass., P.O. 01257** (P.O.,G,L,M 3.3m E; M 0.1m W, 0.8m E)	RGLM	66.3	

Map column: Mass.–Conn. Map 3 — AMC Berkshire Chapter

Massachusetts–Connecticut

GBS	N to S	Features	Facilities	S to N	Map
		Miles from Vt.–Mass. Line		*Miles from Conn.–N.Y. Line*	
	77.3	South Egremont Road (700')	R	64.5	
	79.1	Mass. 41; **South Egremont, Mass., P.O. 01258**			
		(P.O.,L,M 1.2m W)	RLM	62.7	
	80.0	Jug End Road (Curtiss Road)			
		(w 0.3m E)	Rw	61.8	
	81.1	Jug End (1,750')		60.7	
	82.8	Elbow Trail		59.0	
	83.4	Glen Brook Lean-to	Sw	58.4	
	83.5	The Hemlocks Lean-to	Sw	58.3	
	83.9	Guilder Pond Picnic Area	R	57.9	
	84.6	Mt. Everett (2,602')	R	57.2	
	85.3	Race Brook Falls Trail			
		(C,w 0.4m E)	Cw	56.5	
	86.4	Race Mountain		55.4	
	88.2	Laurel Ridge Campsite	Cw	53.6	
	89.5	Sages Ravine (1,340')	w	52.3	
	90.1	Sages Ravine Brook Campsite	Cw	51.7	
	90.2	Massachusetts–Connecticut Line		51.6	
	90.9	Bear Mountain (2,316')		50.9	
	91.6	Bear Mountain Road	R	50.2	
	91.8	Riga Junction, Undermountain Trail		50.0	
	92.3	Brassie Brook (South Branch),			
		Brassie Brook Lean-to	CSw	49.5	
	92.9	Ball Brook Campsite	Cw	48.9	
	93.5	Riga Lean-to	CSw	48.3	
	94.2	Lions Head (1,738')		47.6	
	96.7	Plateau Campsite	Cw	45.1	
	96.9	Conn. 41 (Undermountain Road);			
		Salisbury, Conn., P.O. 06068			
		(P.O.,G,L,M 0.8m W)	RGLM	44.9	

Left margin (top to bottom): Mass. 9 / AMC Berkshire Chapter / Mass. Section 10 / AMC Connecticut Chapter / Conn. Section 1

Right margin: Map 3 / Mass.–Conn. Map 4

Massachusetts–Connecticut

GBS	N to S	Features	Facilities (see page 8 for codes)	S to N	Map
	Miles from Vt.–Mass. Line			*Miles from Conn.–N.Y. Line*	
Conn. Section 2	97.6	U.S. 44 (700')	R	44.2	**Mass.–Conn. Map 4** — *AMC Connecticut Chapter*
	100.1	Billy's View		41.7	
	100.9	Rand's View		40.9	
	101.0	Side trail to Limestone Spring Lean-to (C,S,w 0.5m W)	CSw	40.8	
	101.7	Prospect Mountain (1,475')		40.1	
	104.0	Spring	w	37.8	
	104.5	Housatonic River Road	R	37.3	
	105.1	Iron Bridge over Housatonic River; **Falls Village, Conn., P.O. 06031** (P.O.,M 0.5m E)	RM	36.7	
	107.0	Mohawk Trail (L,M 0.2m E)	LM	34.8	
	107.1	U.S. 7, Housatonic River (500')	R	34.7	
	107.7	U.S. 7, Conn. 112	R	34.1	
	108.1	Belter's Campsite	Cw	33.7	
	110.9	Sharon Mountain Campsite	Cw	30.9	
	112.1	Mt. Easter (1,350')		29.7	
	112.4	Sharon Mountain Road	R	29.4	
Conn. Section 3	113.3	Pine Swamp Brook Lean-to	CSw	28.5	
	114.4	West Cornwall Road (800'); **West Cornwall, Conn., P.O. 06796** (P.O.,M 2.2m E)	RM	27.4	
	114.5	Carse Brook	w	27.3	
	116.7	Caesar Road, Caesar Brook Campsite	C	25.1	
	117.1	Pine Knob Loop Trail		24.7	
	117.8	Hatch Brook		24.0	
	119.0	Old Sharon Road	R	22.8	

Massachusetts–Connecticut

GBS	N to S	Features	Facilities (see page 8 for codes)	S to N	Map
	Miles from Vt.–Mass. Line			*Miles from Conn.–N.Y. Line*	
	119.2	Conn. 4; **Cornwall Bridge, Conn., P.O. 06754** (P.O.,G,L 0.9m E)	RGL	22.6	
	120.1	Silver Hill Campsite (1,000')	Cw	21.7	
	120.9	River Road	Rw	20.9	
	122.9	Stony Brook Campsite	Cw	18.9	
	123.3	Stewart Hollow Brook Lean-to (400')	CSw	18.5	
	125.6	River Road	R	16.2	
	126.1	St. Johns Ledges		15.7	
	126.8	Caleb's Peak (1,160')		15.0	
	127.5	Skiff Mountain Road	R	14.3	
	130.3	Conn. 341, Schaghticoke Road (350'); **Kent, Conn., P.O. 06757** (P.O.,G,L,M 0.8m E)	RGLM	11.5	
	130.6	Mt. Algo Lean-to	CSw	11.2	
	131.6	Thayer Brook		10.2	
	133.5	Schaghticoke Mountain Campsite	Cw	8.3	
	134.1	Indian Rocks		7.7	
	134.5	Connecticut–New York Line (1,250')		7.3	
	135.7	Schaghticoke Mountain		6.1	
	137.4	Schaghticoke Road	R	4.4	
	138.1	Side trail to Bulls Bridge Road Parking Area (R 0.2m E; G,M 0.4m E)	RGM	3.7	
	138.8	Ten Mile River (280')	Cw	3.0	
	139.0	Ten Mile River Lean-to	S	2.8	
	140.0	Ten Mile Hill (1,000')		1.8	
	141.1	Conn. 55	R	0.7	
	141.8	Hoyt Road, Connecticut–New York Line (400'); **Wingdale, N.Y., P.O. 12594** (P.O.,G,M 3.3m W; M 1.5m W, 2.3m W)	RGM	0.0	

Left margin: *New York–New Jersey Trail Conference* | *AMC Connecticut Chapter* — Conn. Section 5 (N.Y. Section 1) | Conn. Section 4

GBS	N to S	Features	Facilities (see page 8 for codes)	S to N	Map

Miles from
Conn.–N.Y. Line

Miles from
Delaware Water Gap, Pa.

	N to S	Features	Facilities	S to N
N.Y. Section 2	0.0	Hoyt Road, Connecticut–New York Line (400'); **Wingdale, N.Y., P.O. 12594** (P.O.,G,M 3.3m W; M 1.5m W, 2.3m W))	RGM	160.9
	1.0	Duell Hollow Road	R	159.9
	1.2	Wiley Shelter	Sw	159.7
	1.6	Leather Hill Road (750')	R	159.3
	6.9	Hurds Corners Road	R	154.0
N.Y. Section 3	7.1	N.Y. 22, Metro-North Railroad, Appalachian Trail Railroad Station (480') (G 0.6m E; L 2.6m W)	RGL	153.8
	9.5	County 20 (West Dover Road); **Pawling, N.Y., P.O. 12564** (P.O.,G,M 2.9m E; C 3.1m E; G 3.2m E; L 4m E)	RCGLM	151.4
	10.2	Telephone Pioneers Shelter	Sw	150.7
	10.5	West Mountain (1,200')		150.4
N.Y. Section 4	14.5	N.Y. 55 (720'); **Poughquag, N.Y., P.O. 12570** (P.O.,M 3.1m W; G 3.6m W; M 1.5m W; L 2.6m W)	RGLM	146.4
	14.8	Old Route 55	R	146.1
	16.7	Depot Hill Road	R	144.2
	17.8	Morgan Stewart Shelter	Sw	143.1
	17.9	Mt. Egbert (1,329')		143.0
	20.3	Stormville Mountain Road, I-84	R	140.6
N.Y. 5	21.7	N.Y. 52 (800'); **Stormville, N.Y., P.O. 12582** (P.O. 1.9m W; G 0.5m E, 2.2m W, 2.4m W; G,M 2m E)	RGM	139.2

N.Y.–N.J. Map 1

New York–New Jersey Trail Conference

New York–New Jersey

Miles from Conn.–N.Y. Line

Miles from Delaware Water Gap, Pa.

	N to S	Features	Facilities	S to N	
N.Y. Section 6 / 5	23.3	Hosner Mountain Road	R	137.6	
	26.5	Taconic State Parkway	R	134.4	
	26.8	Hortontown Road, RPH Shelter (350')	RSw	134.1	
	28.1	Shenandoah Tenting Area	Cw	132.8	
	29.2	Long Hill Road	R	131.7	
	29.6	Shenandoah Mountain (1,282')		131.3	
N.Y. Section 7	33.8	N.Y. 301, Canopus Lake, Fahnestock State Park (C,w 1m E)	RCw	127.1	**N.Y.–N.J. Map 2**
	35.9	Sunk Mine Road (800')	R	125.0	
	37.5	Dennytown Road	RCw	123.4	
	40.2	South Highland Road	R	120.7	
	41.2	Canopus Hill Road (420')	R	119.7	
N.Y. 8	42.9	Old Albany Post Road, Chapman Road	R	118.0	
	43.7	Denning Hill (900')		117.2	
	45.6	Old West Point Road, Graymoor Friary	R	115.3	
N.Y. Section 9	46.2	U.S. 9, N.Y. 403 (400'); **Peekskill, N.Y., P.O. 10566** (P.O.,G,L,M 4.8m E; M 0.7m E; G 1.9m E)	RGLM	114.7	
	49.6	South Mountain Pass (Manitou Road)	R	111.3	
	49.8	Hemlock Springs Campsite	Cw	111.1	
	50.8	Camp Smith Trail, Anthony's Nose (700')		110.1	
	51.3	N.Y. 9D	R	109.6	
N.Y. Section 10	52.0	Bear Mountain Bridge; **Fort Montgomery, N.Y., P.O., 10922** (P.O.,G,L,M, 0.7m W)	RGLM	108.9	**N.Y.–N.J. Map 3**
	52.1	Trailside Museum and Zoo (124')		108.8	
	52.8	Bear Mountain Inn, **Bear Mountain, N.Y., P.O. 10911** (P.O. 0.3m E; L,M,w on A.T.)	RLMw	108.1	

New York–New Jersey Trail Conference

New York–New Jersey

Miles from Conn.–N.Y. Line · *Miles from Delaware Water Gap, Pa.*

	N to S	Features	Facilities	S to N	
N.Y. Section 10	54.6	Bear Mountain (1,305')	Rw	106.3	
	56.2	Seven Lakes Drive	R	104.7	
	57.8	Trail to West Mountain Shelter (S 0.6m E)	S(nw)	103.1	
	58.6	Beechy Bottom Brook	w	102.3	
	58.8	Palisades Interstate Parkway (680')	R	102.1	
	59.5	Black Mountain (1,160')		101.4	
	60.9	William Brien Memorial Shelter	S(nw)	100.0	
N.Y. Section 11	62.1	Goshen Mountain		98.8	
	62.9	Seven Lakes Drive	R	98.0	
	65.1	Arden Valley Road (1,196') (w 0.3m E)	Rw	95.8	
	66.2	Fingerboard Shelter	S(nw)	94.7	
	67.2	Surebridge Mountain		93.7	
	68.3	Lemon Squeezer		92.6	
	68.9	Island Pond Outlet	w	92.0	
	70.2	Arden Valley Road	R	90.7	
	70.4	New York State Thruway (560')		90.5	
N.Y. Section 12	70.6	N.Y. 17; **Arden, N.Y., P.O. 10910; Southfields, N.Y., P.O. 10975** (P.O. 0.7m W; P.O.,L,M 2.1m E; G 1.8m E, 5.7m E)	RGLM	90.3	
	71.7	Arden Mountain (1,180')		89.2	
	72.4	Orange Turnpike (w 0.5m E)	Rw	88.5	
	73.1	Little Dam Lake		87.8	
	73.8	East Mombasha Road	R	87.1	
	74.6	Buchanan Mountain (1,142')		86.3	
	75.5	West Mombasha Road (G 0.6m W)	RG	85.4	

N.Y.–N.J. Map 3

New York–New Jersey Trail Conference

New York–New Jersey

	Miles from Conn.–N.Y. Line			*Miles from Delaware Water Gap, Pa.*	
	76.7	Mombasha High Point (1,280')		84.2	
	78.7	Fitzgerald Falls	w	82.2	
	79.0	Lakes Road (680')	R	81.9	
	80.5	Wildcat Shelter	Sw	80.4	
	80.8	Cat Rocks		80.1	
	81.3	Eastern Pinnacles (1,294')		79.6	
	82.6	N.Y. 17A; **Bellvale, N.Y., P.O. 10912; Greenwood Lake, N.Y., P.O. 10925** (P.O.,G 1.6m W; P.O.,G,L,M 2m E; G,L,M 3.5m W)	RGLM	78.3	
	88.1	Prospect Rock (1,433')		72.8	
	88.5	State Line Trail, New York–New Jersey Line; **Hewitt, N.J., P.O. 07421** (P.O.,G,M 3.7m E)	GM	72.4	
	89.6	Long House Creek		71.3	
	90.7	Long House Road (Brady Road) (G,M 0.7m W)	RGM	70.2	
	92.1	Warwick Turnpike (1,140') (G 1.8m E, 2.7m W; L,M 0.8m W; M 1.5m E)	RGLM	68.8	
	92.5	Wawayanda Shelter (S on A.T.; w 0.4m E)	Sw	68.4	
	92.7	Wawayanda Road	R	68.2	
	93.6	Iron Mountain Road Bridge	R	67.3	
	94.7	Barrett Road; **New Milford, N.Y., P.O. 10959** (P.O.,G 1.8m W)	RG	66.2	
	96.4	Wawayanda Mountain (1,340')		64.5	

Left margin (vertical): *New York–New Jersey Trail Conference*

Left margin boxes (vertical): N.Y. Section 12 | N.Y. Section 13 | N.J. Section 1

Right margin boxes (vertical): N.Y.–N.J. Map 3 | N.Y.–N.J. Map 4

New York–New Jersey

Miles from Conn.–N.Y. Line *Miles from Delaware Water Gap, Pa.*

	N to S	Features	Facilities	S to N	
	97.8	N.J. 94 (450'); **Vernon, N.J., P.O. 07462** (P.O.,G,M 2.4m E)	RGM	63.1	
	98.7	Canal Road	R	62.2	
	99.4	Pochuck Creek footbridge		61.5	
	100.1	County 517	R	60.8	
	101.6	County 565; **Glenwood, N.J., P.O. 07418** (P.O. 0.7m W; L 1m W)	RL	59.3	
	102.8	Pochuck Mountain (800')		58.1	
	104.3	Pochuck Mountain Shelter	S(nw)	56.6	
	104.8	Lake Wallkill Road (Liberty Corners Road)	Rw	56.1	
	107.1	Wallkill River	R	53.8	
	108.1	Oil City Road	R	52.8	
	108.6	N.J. 284 (420') (G 0.4m W)	RG	52.3	
	109.6	Lott Road; **Unionville, N.Y., P.O. 10988** (P.O.,G,M 0.4m W)	RGM	51.3	
	110.5	Unionville Road	R	50.4	
	112.8	Gemmer Road	R	48.1	
	115.4	County 519	R	45.5	
	116.7	High Point Shelter	Sw	44.2	
	117.2	Side trail to High Point Monument		43.7	
	118.4	N.J. 23 (1,500') (w on A.T.; G 2.5m E, 4.3m W; L 1.4m E, 4.4m W; M 4.3m W)	RGLMw	42.5	
	121.0	Trail to Rutherford Shelter (S,w 0.4m E)	Sw	39.9	
	123.7	Deckertown Turnpike	R	37.2	

Left margin labels: N.J. Section 2, N.J. Section 3, N.J. Section 4

Right margin labels: N.Y.–N.J. Map 4, N.Y.–N.J. Map 5, New York–New Jersey Trail Conference

New York–New Jersey

		Miles from Conn.–N.Y. Line	*Miles from Delaware Water Gap, Pa.*		
	123.9	Mashipacong Shelter	S	37.0	
	126.5	Crigger Road	R	34.4	
	127.3	Sunrise Mountain (1,653')	R	33.6	
	129.7	Trail to Gren Anderson Shelter	Sw	31.2	
	130.8	Culver Fire Tower		30.1	
	132.7	Culvers Gap, U.S. 206 (935'); **Branchville, N.J., P.O. 07826** (P.O. 3.4m E; G on A.T., 1.6m E; L 2.5m E, 1.9m W; M 0.1m W, 0.6m E)	RGLM	28.2	
	136.3	Brink Road Shelter (S,w 0.2m W)	Sw	24.6	
	138.5	Rattlesnake Mountain (1,492')		22.4	
	140.4	Buttermilk Falls Trail		20.5	
	143.3	Blue Mountain Lakes Road	Rw	17.6	
	147.2	Millbrook–Blairstown Road (1,260')	R	13.7	
	147.6	Rattlesnake Spring	w	13.3	
	148.2	Catfish Fire Tower (1,565')		12.7	
	150.6	Camp Road, Mohican Outdoor Center (C,L,w 0.3m W)	RCLw	10.3	
	154.9	Spring	w	6.0	
	155.0	Sunfish Pond (1,382')		5.9	
	156.3	Backpacker Site	C(nw)	4.6	
	157.9	Holly Springs Trail (w 0.2m E)	w	3.0	
	159.5	I-80 Overpass	R	1.4	
	159.9	Delaware Water Gap National Recreation Area Information Center	Rw	1.0	
	160.9	Delaware River Bridge (west end), New Jersey–Pennsylvania Line (350')	R	0.0	

Left margin: *New York–New Jersey Trail Conference* — N.J. Section 4 / N.J. Section 5 / N.J. Section 6

Right margin: N.Y.–N.J. Map 5 / N.Y.–N.J. Map 6

Pennsylvania

GBS	N to S	Features	Facilities (see page 8 for codes)	S to N	Map

Miles from
Delaware Water Gap, Pa.

Miles from
Pa.–Md. Line

Pa. Section 1	0.0	Delaware River Bridge (west end), New Jersey–Pennsylvania Line (350')	R	229.3	*Wilmington Trail Club*
	0.2	Pa. 611, **Delaware Water Gap, Pa., P.O. 18327** (P.O.,M 0.1m W; L,M 0.4m W; G,L 3.2m W)	RGLM	229.1	
	0.9	Council Rock		228.4	
	1.7	Lookout Rock		227.6	
	2.7	Mt. Minsi (1,461')		226.6	
	4.7	Totts Gap		224.6	
	6.6	Kirkridge Shelter (1,500')	Sw	222.7	
	7.2	Fox Gap, Pa. 191	R	222.1	
	8.8	Wolf Rocks		220.5	
	15.8	Pa. 33 (980'); **Wind Gap, Pa., P.O. 18091** (P.O.,G,L,M 1m E; L 0.1m W)	RGLM	213.5	
Pa. Section 2	16.8	Hahns Lookout		212.5	
	20.4	Leroy A. Smith Shelter (S 0.1m E; w 0.2m E)	Sw	208.9	
	23.9	Smith Gap Road	R	205.4	
	24.6	Spring (w 0.5m E)	w	204.7	
	26.4	Delps Trail (1,580')		202.9	
	31.2	Little Gap (1,100'); **Danielsville, Pa., P.O. 18038** (P.O.,G,M 1.5m E; w 1.2m W)	RGMw	198.1	
	36.2	Pa. 248	R	193.1	
	36.4	Lehigh River Bridge (east end), Pa. 873 (380'); **Palmerton, Pa., P.O. 18071** (P.O.,G,L,M 2m W)	RGLM	192.9	

KTA Sections 1–6 Map

Batona

AMC Delaware Valley Chapter

Philadelphia Trail Club

Pennsylvania

GBS	N to S	Features	Facilities (see page 8 for codes)	S to N	Map
	Miles from *Delaware Water Gap, Pa.*		*Miles from* *Pa.–Md. Line*		
	36.5	Lehigh Gap, Pa. 873; **Slatington, Pa., P.O. 18080** (P.O.,G,L,M 2m E)	RGLM	192.8	
	37.1	George W. Outerbridge Shelter	Sw	192.2	
	41.5	Ashfield Road, Lehigh Furnace Gap (1,320'); **Ashfield, Pa., P.O. 18212** (P.O.,G 2.2m W; w 0.7m E)	RGw	187.8	
	43.9	Bake Oven Knob Shelter	Sw	185.4	
	44.5	Bake Oven Knob (1,560')		184.8	
	44.9	Bake Oven Knob Road	R	184.4	
	46.3	Bear Rocks		183.0	
	47.0	The Cliffs		182.3	
	48.0	New Tripoli Campsite (C,w 0.2m W)	Cw	181.3	
	49.8	Pa. 309, Blue Mountain Summit (1,360') (L,M,w on A.T.)	RLMw	179.5	
	52.0	Fort Franklin Road	R	177.3	
	53.9	Allentown Hiking Club Shelter	Sw	175.4	
	55.2	Tri-County Corner (1,560')		174.1	
	61.3	Hawk Mountain Road, Eckville Shelter (600') (S,w 0.2m E)	RSw	168.0	
	66.6	The Pinnacle		162.7	
	67.0	Trail to Blue Rocks Campground (C,G,S 1.5m E)	CGS	162.3	
	68.8	Pulpit Rock (1,582')		160.5	
	70.4	Windsor Furnace Shelter (940')	Sw	158.9	

Left margin (top to bottom): Philadelphia TC · Blue Mtn. Eagle · Allentown Hiking Club · Blue Mtn. Eagle Climbing Club

Inner left margin: Pa. Section 3 · Pa. Section 4

Right margin: KTA Sections 1–6 Map

Pennsylvania

Blue Mountain Eagle Climbing Club (BMECC)

KTA Sections 1–6 Map

GBS	N to S	Features	Facilities (see page 8 for codes)	S to N	Map
		Miles from *Delaware Water Gap, Pa.*		*Miles from* *Pa.–Md. Line*	
Pa. Section 4	70.6	Windsor Furnace	Cw	158.7	
	73.2	Pocahontas Spring (1,200') (C,w on A.T.; L,M 1m E)	CLMw	156.1	
	75.8	Pa. 61 (M 0.5m W)	RM	153.5	
	76.5	**Port Clinton, Pa., P.O. 19549** (400') (P.O. on A.T.; L,S 0.5m W; G,M,L 3m E)	RGLMS	152.8	
Pa. Section 5	80.5	Phillip's Canyon Spring (1,500')	w	148.8	
	83.2	Shartlesville Cross-Mountain Road; **Shartlesville, Pa., P.O. 19554** (P.O.,G,L,M 3.6m E)	RGLM	146.1	
	85.1	Eagle's Nest Shelter (S,w 0.3m W)	Sw	144.2	
	85.8	Sand Spring Trail (w 0.2m E)	w	143.5	
	89.6	Black Swatara Spring (w 0.3m E)	w	139.7	
	90.9	Pa. 183, Rentschler Marker (1,440')	R	138.4	
	91.2	Fort Dietrich Snyder Marker (w 0.2m W)	w	138.1	
	94.5	Shuberts Gap		134.8	
Pa. Section 6	94.6	Hertlein Campsite	Cw	134.7	
	97.1	Round Head and Shower Steps	w	132.2	
	99.7	Trail to Pilger Ruh Spring	Cw	129.6	
	100.2	Pa. 501; **Pine Grove, Pa., P.O. 17963,** 501 Shelter (P.O.,M 3.7m W; S,w 0.1m W; G 4.3m W; L 5.7m W)	RGLMSw	129.1	
	102.1	Pa. 645	R	127.2	

Pennsylvania

GBS	N to S	Features	Facilities (see page 8 for codes)	S to N	Map

Miles from
Delaware Water Gap, Pa.

Miles from
Pa.–Md. Line

	N to S	Features	Facilities	S to N	
Pa.6	104.3	Blue Mountain Spring, William Penn Shelter (1,380')	Sw	125.0	**1-6 Map**
	111.2	I-81	R	118.1	
	111.6	Swatara Gap, Pa. 72 (480') (C,G,L,M 2m E)	RGL	117.7	
Pa. Section 7	113.0	Pa. 443; Green Point, Pa.	R	116.3	
	117.6	Rausch Gap Shelter (980') (S,w 0.3m E)	Sw	111.7	
	119.9	Cold Spring Trail		109.4	
	122.2	Yellow Springs Village Site		107.1	
	125.6	Stony Mountain; Horse-Shoe Trail (1,650')		103.7	KTA Sections 7–8 Map
Pa. Section 8	128.6	Pa. 325, Clarks Valley (550')	Rw	100.7	
	129.0	Spring	w	100.3	
	132.5	Shikellimy Overlook (1,320')		96.8	
	135.1	Peters Mountain Shelter	Sw	94.2	
	136.0	Table Rock		93.3	
	138.0	Pa. 225 overpass	R	91.3	
	141.9	Clarks Ferry Shelter (1,260')	Sw	87.4	
	144.6	U.S. 22 & 322, Norfolk Southern Railway	R	84.7	
Pa. Section 9	145.2	Clarks Ferry Bridge (west end), Susquehanna River (380') (C on A.T.; M 0.1m W)	RCM	84.1	
	145.4	Juniata River, Pa. 849	R	83.9	
	146.4	**Duncannon, Pa., P.O. 17020** (P.O.,L,M on A.T., G 0.6m W)	RGLM	82.9	PATC Map 1
	146.9	U.S. 11 & 15, Pa. 274	R	82.4	
	148.6	Hawk Rock		80.7	
	150.5	Cove Mountain Shelter (1,200')	Sw	78.8	
	155.5	Pa. 850 (650')	R	73.8	

Side labels (left margin): BMECC — Susquehanna A.T. Club — York — Mountain Club of Maryland

Pennsylvania

GBS	N to S	Features	Facilities (see page 8 for codes)	S to N	Map

Miles from
Delaware Water Gap, Pa.

Miles from
Pa.–Md. Line

	N to S	Features	Facilities	S to N	
Pa. 9	157.8	Darlington Shelter (1,250')	Sw	71.5	
	157.9	Darlington Trail, Tuscarora Trail		71.4	
	158.8	Spring	w	70.5	
	159.8	Pa. 944 (480'); Donnellytown, Pa.	R	69.5	
Pa. Section 10	161.8	Conodoguinet Creek, Scott Farm Trail Work Center	Rw	67.5	
	163.2	I-81 Crossing	R	66.1	
	164.1	U.S. 11; **Carlisle, Pa., P.O. 17013** **New Kingston, Pa., P.O. 17072** (P.O. 5m W; 1.7m E; G 1.3m E; L,M 0.3m W; M 0.3m E)	RGLM	65.2	
	165.3	Pennsylvania Turnpike	R	64.0	
	168.0	Trindle Road (Pa. 641)	R	61.3	
	170.1	Pa. 74	R	59.2	
Pa. Section 11	172.1	Pa. 174, ATC Mid-Atlantic Regional Office; **Boiling Springs, Pa., P.O. 17007** (P.O.,w on A.T.; G,L,M 0.1m W; G 1m W)	RGLMw	57.2	
	172.4	Yellow Breeches Creek (500')	RC	56.9	
	175.1	Center Point Knob (1,060')		54.2	
	176.0	Alec Kennedy Shelter	Sw	53.3	
	178.1	Whiskey Spring, Whiskey Spring Road	Rw	51.2	
Pa. Section 12	180.9	Pa. 94 (880'); **Mount Holly Springs, Pa., P.O. 17065** (P.O.,G,M 2.5m W)	RGM	48.4	
	182.9	Hunters Run Road (Pa. 34); **Gardners, Pa., P.O. 17324** (P.O. 5m E; G 0.2m E)	RG	46.4	
	183.8	Pine Grove Road (C,M 0.4m W)	RCM	45.5	

Cumberland Valley A.T. Club — PATC Map 1

Mountain Club of Maryland — PATC Maps 2–3

Pennsylvania

GBS	N to S	Features	Facilities (see page 8 for codes)	S to N	Map
	Miles from Delaware Water Gap, Pa.			*Miles from Pa.–Md. Line*	
Potomac A.T. Club / Mountain Club of Maryland; Pa. Section 12	184.3	James Fry (Tagg Run) Shelter (S,w 0.2m E)	Sw	45.0	PATC Maps 2–3
	185.5	Side trail to Mountain Creek Campground (C,G 0.7m W)	CG	43.8	
	185.7	Limekiln Road	R	43.6	
	189.0	Side trail to Pole Steeple (1,300')		40.3	
	191.5	Pine Grove Furnace State Park	RCGLw	37.8	
Pa. Section 13	191.8	Pa. 233 (900')	R	37.5	
	195.2	Toms Run Shelters	Sw	34.1	
	196.3	Woodrow Road	R	33.0	
	198.2	Michener Cabin (locked) (w 0.3m E)	w	31.1	
	200.1	Shippensburg Road, Big Flat Fire Tower (2,040')	R	29.2	
	201.4	Birch Run Shelter	Sw	27.9	
	203.8	Milesburn Road, Milesburn Cabin (locked)	Rw	25.5	
	204.2	Ridge Road, Means Hollow Road	R	25.1	
	204.7	Middle Ridge Road	R	24.6	
	207.3	Sandy Sod Junction (1,980')	R	22.0	
	208.8	Quarry Gap Shelters	Sw	20.5	
	209.5	Quarry Gap Road	R	19.8	
Pa. Section 14	211.4	U.S. 30, Caledonia State Park, Thaddeus Stevens Museum (960'); **Fayetteville, Pa., P.O. 17222** (P.O.,G,L,M 3.5m W; C,w on A.T.; M 0.5m W; G 0.9m W)	RCGLMw	17.9	

Pennsylvania

	N to S	Features	Facilities (see page 8 for codes)	S to N	
	Miles from Delaware Water Gap, Pa.			*Miles from Pa.–Md. Line*	
	214.4	Rocky Mountain Shelters (S 0.2m E; w 0.5m E)	Sw	14.9	
	216.1	Pa. 233 (1,600'); **South Mountain, Pa., P.O. 17261** (P.O.,G 1.2m E)	RG	13.2	
	216.4	Swamp Road	R	12.9	
	219.7	Chimney Rocks (1,900')		9.6	
	221.0	Tumbling Run Shelters, Hermitage Cabin (locked)	Sw	8.3	
Pa. Section 14	221.2	Old Forge Road (1,000')	R	8.1	PATC Map 4 / Potomac A.T. Club
	221.8	Rattlesnake Run Road	R	7.5	
	222.2	Antietam Shelter, Old Forge Park	RSw	7.1	
	224.6	Deer Lick Shelters (1,420')	Sw	4.7	
	225.9	Bailey Spring	w	3.4	
	226.5	Mackie Run, Mentzer Gap Road	R	2.8	
	226.7	Pa. 16; **Blue Ridge Summit, Pa., P.O. 17214** (P.O.,G,M 1.2m E; G 2.6m W)	RGM	2.6	
	227.0	Old Pa. 16	R	2.3	
	228.2	Buena Vista Road	Rw	1.1	
	229.2	Pen Mar Road	R	0.1	
	229.3	Pennsylvania–Maryland Line (1,250')	R	0.0	

GBS	N to S	Features	Facilities (see page 8 for codes)	S to N	Map

Miles from Pa.–Md. Line

Miles from Front Royal, Va.

Potomac A.T. Club

	N to S	Features	Facilities	S to N
Md. Section 1	0.0	Pennsylvania–Maryland Line (1,250')	R	94.9
	0.2	Pen Mar Park;		
		Cascade, Md., P.O. 21719		
		(P.O.,G,M 1.6m E; w on A.T.;		
		M 1.4m E)	RGMw	94.7
	3.1	Trail to High Rock	R	91.8
	4.9	Devils Racecourse Shelter Trail		
		(C,S,w 0.3m E)	CSw	90.0
Md. 2	5.9	Raven Rock Hollow, Md. 491	R	89.0
	6.7	Warner Gap Road	Rw	88.2
	8.5	Foxville Road (Md. 77)	R	86.4
	9.8	Ensign Cowall Shelter	Sw	85.1
Md. Section 3	10.0	Wolfsville Road (Md. 17) (1,400');		
		Smithsburg, Md., P.O. 21783		
		(P.O.,G,M 2.4m W; L 6.4m W)	RGLM	84.9
	14.7	Pogo Memorial Campsite	Cw	80.2
	15.4	Black Rock Cliffs (1,800')		79.5
	16.4	Trail to Annapolis Rock		
		(w 0.2m W)	Cw	78.5
	18.0	Pine Knob Shelter	CSw	76.9
	18.6	I-70 Footbridge, U.S. 40		
		(C 1.4m W; M,w 0.4m W)	RCMw	76.3
Md. Section 4	19.4	Boonsboro Mountain Road	R	75.5
	21.5	Washington Monument		73.4
	21.9	Washington Monument Road	Rw	73.0
	22.1	Monument Road	R	72.8
	23.5	Turners Gap, U.S. Alt. 40 (1,000');		
		Boonsboro, Md., P.O. 21713		
		(M on A.T; P.O.,M 2.3m W;		
		G 1.6m W, 3.7m W)	RGM	71.4

PATC Maps 5–6

Maryland–West Virginia–Northern Virginia

GBS	N to S	Features	Facilities (see page 8 for codes)	S to N	Map
	Miles from Pa.–Md. Line			*Miles from Front Royal, Va.*	
	23.7	Dahlgren Back Pack Campground	Cw	71.2	
	24.5	Reno Monument Road	R	70.4	
	25.5	Rocky Run Shelter			
		(C,S,w 0.2m W)	CSw	69.4	
Md. Section 5	27.1	Lambs Knoll (1,600')		67.8	
	27.3	White Rock Cliff		67.6	
	27.9	Trail to Bear Spring Cabin (locked)			
		(w 0.5m E)	w	67.0	
	30.5	Crampton Gap Shelter			
		(C,S,w 0.3m E)	CSw	64.4	
	30.9	Crampton Gap, Gathland State Park, Gapland Road (Md. 572) (950'); **Burkittsville, Md., P.O. 21718**			
Md. Section 6		(P.O. 1.2m E; w on A.T.)	Rw	64.0	PATC Maps 5–6
	32.6	Brownsville Gap		62.3	Potomac A.T. Club
	34.6	Ed Garvey Shelter			
		(S on A.T.; w 0.4m E)	Sw	60.3	
	36.7	Trail to Weverton Cliffs		58.2	
	37.6	Weverton Road			
		(G 1.4m W)	RG	57.3	
	37.8	U.S. 340 Underpass		57.1	
Md. Section 7	38.0	Keep Tryst Road			
		(L,M 1.2m W)	RLM	56.9	
	38.1	C&O Canal Towpath (east junction)		56.8	
	39.6	U.S. 340, Sandy Hook Bridge		55.3	
	40.7	C&O Canal Towpath (west junction)		54.2	
	40.9	Potomac River, Byron Memorial Footbridge, Maryland–West Virginia Line (250')		54.0	

Maryland–West Virginia–Northern Virginia

Miles from
Pa.–Md. Line

Miles from
Front Royal, Va.

41.0	Shenandoah Street; Harpers Ferry National Historical Park (M 0.1m W)	RM 53.9
41.6	Appalachian Trail Conservancy Side Trail; **Harpers Ferry, W.Va., P.O. 25425** (P.O. 0.5m W; G 1.1m W; L 0.6m W; M 0.4m W; ATC 0.2m W)	RGLM 53.3
41.9	U.S. 340, Shenandoah River Bridge (north end) (L 0.1m W; C 1.2m W)	RCL 53.0
42.9	Chestnut Hill Road (W.Va. 32)	R 52.0
43.5	Loudoun Heights, West Virginia–Virginia Line (1,200')	51.4
47.4	Keys Gap, W.Va. 9 (G,M,w 0.3m W, 0.3m E)	RGMw 47.5
50.4	David Lesser Memorial Shelter (S 0.1m E; w 0.3m E)	Sw 44.5
53.6	Trail to Blackburn Trail Center (1,650') (C 0.1m E; S,w 0.3m E)	CSw 41.3
54.8	Wilson Gap	40.1
57.6	Devils Racecourse	37.3
57.7	Sand Spring	w 37.2
58.3	Crescent Rock	36.6
58.4	West Virginia–Virginia Line	36.5
58.7	Spring	w 36.2
60.9	Snickers Gap, Va. 7, Va. 679 (1,000'); **Bluemont, Va., P.O. 20135** (P.O. 1.7m E; G 1m W; M 0.3m W, 0.9m W)	RGM 34.0

Potomac A.T. Club

W.Va.–Va. Section 1

W.Va.–Va. Section 2

PATC Map 7

Maryland–West Virginia–Northern Virginia

GBS	N to S	Features	Facilities (see page 8 for codes)	S to N	Map
		Miles from Pa.-Md. Line	*Miles from Front Royal, Va.*		
Va. Section 3	61.5	Bears Den Rocks, Bears Den Hostel (L,w 0.2m E)	Lw	33.4	
	64.5	Sawmill Spring, Sam Moore Shelter	Sw	30.4	
	66.5	Spring	w	28.4	
	67.7	Va. 605	R	27.2	
	71.4	Rod Hollow Shelter	Sw	23.5	
Va. Section 4	75.0	Ashby Gap, U.S. 50 (900') (G,M 0.8m W; L 4m W; L,M 1.2m E)	RLM	19.9	PATC Map 8
	77.6	Sky Meadows State Park Side Trail (C,S,w 1.3m E)	CSw	17.3	
	78.8	Spring	w	16.1	
	79.8	Dick's Dome Shelter (S,w 0.2m E)	Sw	15.1	
	82.4	Trico Trail (1,900')		12.5	
	84.2	Manassas Gap Shelter	Sw	10.7	
Va. Section 5	86.7	Va. 55 (800'); **Linden, Va., P.O. 22642** (P.O.,G 1m W)	RG	8.2	
	88.6	Va. 638	R	6.3	
	89.7	Jim & Molly Denton Shelter	CSw	5.2	
	91.6	Tom Sealock Spring (1,800')	w	3.3	
	94.9	U.S. 522 (950'); **Front Royal, Va., P.O. 22630** (P.O.,G 4.2m W; G,M 3.2m W; L,M 3.6m W)	RGLM	0.0	

Potomac A.T. Club

Shenandoah National Park

Miles from
Front Royal, Va.

Miles from
Rockfish Gap, Va.

	N to S	Features	Facilities	S to N
	0.0	U.S. 522 (950'); **Front Royal, Va., P.O. 22630** (P.O.,G 4.2m W; G,M 3.2m W; L,M 3.6m W)	RGLM	107.1
	1.4	Va. 602	R	105.7
	2.9	Tom Floyd Wayside	Sw	104.2
	3.6	Possums Rest Overlook, SNP northern boundary		103.5
	3.8	Compton Gap Fire Road; self-registration station for SNP camping permits		103.3
	5.3	Indian Run Spring (w 0.3m E)	w	101.8
	5.6	Compton Gap; Skyline Drive, mile 10.4	R	101.5
	6.4	Compton Peak (2,909')		100.7
	6.8	Compton Springs	w	100.3
	7.7	Jenkins Gap; Skyline Drive, mile 12.3	R	99.4
	9.4	Hogwallow Gap; Skyline Drive, mile 14.2 (2,739')	R	97.7
	10.0	Hogwallow Spring	w	97.1
	10.9	North Marshall Mountain (3,368')		96.2
	11.6	Skyline Drive, mile 15.9	R	95.5
	12.1	South Marshall Mountain (3,212')		95.0
	13.2	Gravel Springs Gap; Skyline Drive, mile 17.7 (2,666')	R	93.9
	13.4	Gravel Springs Hut (S,w 0.2m E)	Sw	93.7
	14.5	Skyline Drive, mile 18.9	R	92.6
	15.0	Little Hogback Mountain		92.1
	15.1	Little Hogback Overlook; Skyline Drive, mile 19.7	R	92.0

Potomac A.T. Club

SNP Section 1 (Va. 6)

SNP Section 2 (Va. 7)

PATC Map 9

Shenandoah National Park

	N to S	Features	Facilities (see page 8 for codes)	S to N	Map

Miles from Front Royal, Va.

Miles from Rockfish Gap, Va.

	N to S	Features	Facilities	S to N	Map
	15.8	First peak of Hogback		91.3	
	15.9	Spring			
		(w 0.2m E)	w	91.2	
	16.1	Second peak of Hogback (3,475')		91.0	
	16.3	Skyline Drive, mile 20.8	R	90.8	
	16.4	Third peak of Hogback		90.7	
	16.6	Skyline Drive, mile 21.1	R	90.5	
	17.0	Tuscarora Trail		90.1	
	17.6	Rattlesnake Point Overlook;			
		Skyline Drive, mile 21.9	R	89.5	
SNP Section 2 (Va.7)	18.3	Range View Cabin (locked)	w	88.8	
		(w 0.1m E)			
	19.1	Elkwallow Gap;			
		Skyline Drive, mile 23.9 (2,480')			PATC Map 9
		(G,M 0.1m E)	RGLM	88.0	
	19.6	Spring	w	87.5	
	24.2	Byrds Nest #4 Picnic Shelter			
		(0.5m E)	w	82.9	
	24.3	Beahms Gap; Skyline Drive, mile 28.5	R	82.8	
	24.6	Skyline Drive, mile 28.6	R	82.5	
	25.7	Pass Mountain (3,052')		81.4	
	26.5	Pass Mountain Hut			
		(S,w 0.2m E)	Sw	80.6	
SNP Section 3 (Va.8)	27.7	Thornton Gap, U.S. 211;			
		Skyline Drive, mile 31.5 (2,307')	R	79.4	
	29.6	Marys Rock (3,514')		77.5	PATC Map 10
	30.2	Meadow Spring			
		(w 0.3m E)	w	76.9	
	30.9	Byrds Nest #3 Picnic Shelter		76.2	
	31.9	The Pinnacle (3,730')		75.2	

Potomac A.T. Club

Shenandoah National Park

GBS	N to S	Features	Facilities (see page 8 for codes)	S to N	Map
	Miles from Front Royal, Va.			*Miles from Rockfish Gap, Va.*	
	32.9	Side trail to Jewell Hollow Overlook; Skyline Drive, mile 36.4	R	74.2	
	33.0	Pinnacles Picnic Ground; Skyline Drive, mile 36.7	Rw	74.1	
	35.2	Hughes River Gap; side trail to Stony Man Mountain Overlook; Skyline Drive, mile 38.6 (3,097')	Rw	71.9	
	36.8	Side trail to Stony Man summit		70.3	
	37.2	Skyland Service Road (north) (L,M 0.3m W)	RLM	69.9	
	38.0	Skyland Service Road (south)	R	69.1	
	40.1	Side trail to Crescent Rock Overlook; Skyline Drive, mile 44.4	R	67.0	
	40.5	Hawksbill Gap; Skyline Drive, mile 45.6 (3,361')	R	66.6	
	41.5	Side trail to Hawksbill Mountain, Byrd's Nest #2 Picnic Shelter (0.9m E)		65.6	
	41.8	Rock Spring Cabin (locked) & Hut (S,w 0.2m W)	Sw	65.3	
	43.7	Fishers Gap; Skyline Drive, mile 49.3	R	63.4	
	44.7	David Spring	w	62.4	
	45.3	Big Meadows (3,500') (C,L,M 0.1m E)	RCLM	61.8	
	46.2	Big Meadows Wayside, Harry F. Byrd, Sr., Visitor Center (w on A.T.; G,M 0.4m E)	RGMw	60.9	
	47.0	Spring	w	60.1	
	47.9	Milam Gap; Skyline Drive, mile 52.8	R	59.2	
	49.8	Hazeltop (3,812')		57.3	

Left margin (top to bottom): Potomac A.T. Club — SNP Section 3 (Va. 8) — SNP Section 4 (Va. 9) — SNP Section 5 (Va. 10)

Right margin: PATC Map 10

Shenandoah National Park

GBS	N to S	Features	Facilities (see page 8 for codes)	S to N	Map

Miles from Front Royal, Va.   *Miles from Rockfish Gap, Va.*

50.7	Bootens Gap; Skyline Drive, mile 55.1 (3,243')	R	56.4	
53.3	Bearfence Mountain Hut (S,w 0.1m E)	Sw	53.8	
54.0	Lewis Mountain Campground; Skyline Drive, mile 57.6 (C,G,L,w 0.1m W)	RCGLw	53.1	
55.7	Spring	w	51.4	
56.0	Pocosin Cabin (locked)	w	51.1	
59.3	South River Picnic Grounds (w 0.1m W)	w	47.8	
62.3	Swift Run Gap, U.S. 33; Skyline Drive, mile 65.5 (2,367')	R	44.8	
63.6	Skyline Drive, mile 66.7	R	43.5	
65.1	Hightop Mountain (3,587')		42.0	
65.2	Spring	w	41.9	
65.7	Hightop Hut (S 0.1m W; w 0.2m W)	Sw	41.4	
66.9	Smith Roach Gap; Skyline Drive, mile 68.6	R	40.2	
68.1	Little Roundtop Mountain		39.0	
68.5	Powell Gap; Skyline Drive, mile 69.9 (2,294')	R	38.6	
71.8	Simmons Gap; Skyline Drive, mile 73.2	Rw	35.3	
73.7	Pinefield Gap; Skyline Drive, mile 75.2	R	33.4	
73.9	Pinefield Hut	Sw	33.2	
75.5	Ivy Creek Overlook; Skyline Drive, mile 77.5	R	31.6	
77.6	Spring (w 0.1m W)	w	29.5	

SNP Section 5 (Va. 10) / SNP Section 6 (Va. 11) / SNP Section 7 (Va.12)

PATC Map 10 / PATC Map 11 / Potomac A.T. Club

Shenandoah National Park

GBS	N to S	Features	Facilities	S to N	Map
	79.7	Loft Mountain Campground (3,300') (C,G,M,w 0.2m W)	CGMw	27.4	
	81.8	Doyles River Cabin (locked); Skyline Drive, mile 81.1 (w 0.3m E)	Rw	25.3	
	82.7	Doyles River Parking Overlook; Skyline Drive, mile 81.9	R	24.4	
	83.1	Skyline Drive, mile 82.2	R	24.0	
	84.0	Browns Gap; Skyline Drive, mile 82.9 (2,600')	R	23.1	
	85.5	Skyline Drive, mile 84.3	R	21.6	
	86.5	Blackrock (3,100')		20.6	
	87.1	Blackrock Hut (S,w 0.2m E)	Sw	20.0	
	87.6	Skyline Drive, mile 87.2	R	19.5	
	87.8	Blackrock Gap; Skyline Drive, mile 87.4 (2,321')	R	19.3	
	89.6	Skyline Drive, mile 88.9	R	17.5	
	93.7	Skyline Drive, mile 92.4 (3,100')	R	13.4	
	95.7	Turk Gap; Skyline Drive, mile 94.1	R	11.4	
	97.3	Skyline Drive, mile 95.3	R	9.8	
	98.9	Spring	w	8.2	
	99.1	Jarman Gap; Skyline Drive, mile 96.9; SNP southern boundary (2,173')	R	8.0	
	99.5	Spring	w	7.6	
	100.1	Calf Mountain Shelter (w 0.2m W; S 0.3m W)	Sw	7.0	
	101.6	Beagle Gap; Skyline Drive, mile 99.5	R	5.5	
	102.1	Bear Den Mountain (2,885')		5.0	
	103.4	McCormick Gap; Skyline Drive, mile 102.1	R	3.7	

Left margin labels: Potomac A.T. Club — SNP Section 7 (Va.12), SNP Section 8 (Va.13), SNP Section 9 (Va.14)

Right margin label: PATC Map 11

Shenandoah National Park

SNP Section 9 (Va.14)

GBS	N to S	Features	Facilities (see page 8 for codes)	S to N	Map

Miles from Front Royal, Va.

Miles from Rockfish Gap, Va.

N to S	Features	Facilities	S to N
106.3	Self-registration for SNP camping permits, park entrance station (0.2m W)		0.8
106.8	Skyline Drive, mile 105.2	R	0.3
107.0	I-64 Overpass		0.1
107.1	Rockfish Gap, U.S. 250, I-64 (1,902'); **Waynesboro, Va., P.O. 22980** (P.O.,G,L,M 4.5m W; G,L,M on A.T.)	RGLM	0.0

PATC Map 11

Potomac A.T. Club

GBS	N to S	Features	Facilities (see page 8 for codes)	S to N	Map

Miles from Rockfish Gap, Va.   *Miles from New River, Va.*

	N to S	Features	Facilities	S to N
	0.0	Rockfish Gap, U.S. 250, I-64 (1,902'); **Waynesboro, Va., P.O. 22980** (P.O.,G,L,M 4.5m W; G,L,M on A.T.)	RGLM	225.8
	5.0	Mill Creek, Paul C. Wolfe Shelter	Sw	220.8
	6.5	Side trail to Humpback Visitors Center (w 1.3m W)	w	219.3
	7.9	Glass Hollow Overlook		217.9
	9.1	Bear Spring	w	216.7
	10.8	Humpback Mountain; side trail to Humpback Rocks		215.0
	14.6	Dripping Rock Parking Area; Blue Ridge Parkway, mile 9.6	Rw	211.2
	15.0	Cedar Cliff		210.8
	18.9	Three Ridges Parking Overlook; Blue Ridge Parkway, mile 13.1	R	206.9
	19.4	Reeds Gap, Va. 664; Blue Ridge Parkway, mile 13.6	R	206.4
	21.1	Maupin Field Shelter	Sw	204.7
	23.1	Hanging Rock Overlook		202.7
	24.0	Three Ridges (3,870')		201.8
	25.3	Chimney Rocks		200.5
	27.3	Harpers Creek Shelter	Sw	198.5
	29.9	Tye River, Va. 56 (970') (C,w on A.T.; G 2m E; C,G 4m W)	RCG	195.9
	31.2	Cripple Creek	w	194.6
	34.2	The Priest (4,063')		191.6
	34.7	The Priest Shelter	Sw	191.1
	35.6	Crabtree Farm Road (Va. 826), Crabtree Falls Trail (C,w 0.5m W)	RCw	190.2

Side labels (left margin, top to bottom): Old Dominion A.T. Club — Va. Section 15; Tidewater A.T. Club — Va. Section 16; Natural Bridge A.T. Club — Va. Section 17

Side label (right margin): Va. Map 5

Central Virginia

GBS	N to S	Features	Facilities	S to N	Map
	Miles from Rockfish Gap, Va.			*Miles from New River, Va.*	
Va. 17	36.4	Cash Hollow Road (3,280')	R	189.4	
	37.7	Cash Hollow Rock		188.1	
	38.5	Main Top Mountain (4,040')		187.3	
	38.8	Spy Rock		187.0	
Va. Section 18	39.3	Fish Hatchery Road (3,454'); **Montebello, Va., P.O. 24464** (P.O. 2.5m W; C,G,L 2.2m W)	RCGL	186.5	Va. Map 5
	40.5	Porters Field	Cw	185.3	
	41.6	Seeley-Woodworth Shelter	Sw	184.2	
	42.3	Elk Pond Branch	Cw	183.5	
	43.5	North Fork of Piney River	Cw	182.3	
	45.4	Greasy Spring Road	R	180.4	
	45.9	USFS 246	R	179.9	
	47.1	Salt Log Gap (north), USFS 63 (3,257')	R	178.7	
Va. Section 19	48.4	Tar Jacket Ridge (3,847')		177.4	
	49.3	Hog Camp Gap, USFS 48 (3,485')	RCw	176.5	
	50.6	Cold Mountain (4,022')		175.2	
	51.8	Old Hotel Trail, Cow Camp Gap Shelter (3,428') (S,w 0.6m E)	Sw	174.0	
	52.8	Bald Knob (4,059')		173.0	
Va. Section 20	55.6	U.S. 60 (2,065'); **Buena Vista, Va., P.O. 24416** (P.O.,G,L,M 9.3m W)	RGLM	170.2	
	57.4	Brown Mountain Creek Shelter	Sw	168.4	
	59.4	Pedlar Lake Road (USFS 38)	R	166.4	
	62.4	Pedlar River Bridge, USFS 39, Little Irish Creek	RCw	163.4	
	64.3	Rice Mountain (2,228')		161.5	
	66.2	Robinson Gap Road (Va. 607)	R	159.6	

Natural Bridge A.T. Club

Central Virginia

GBS	N to S	Features	Facilities (see page 8 for codes)	S to N	Map
	Miles from Rockfish Gap, Va.			*Miles from New River, Va.*	
Va. Section 21	66.5	Blue Ridge Parkway, mile 51.7; Punchbowl Mountain Crossing (2,170')	Rw	159.3	Va. Map 5
	66.9	Punchbowl Shelter (S,w 0.2m W)	Sw	158.9	
	67.4	Punchbowl Mountain		158.4	
	68.5	Bluff Mountain (3,372')		157.3	
	70.0	Saltlog Gap (south) (2,573')		155.8	
	71.1	Saddle Gap, Saddle Gap Trail		154.7	
	72.6	Big Rocky Row (2,992')		153.2	
	73.6	Fullers Rocks, Little Rocky Row (2,472')		152.2	
	73.7	Rocky Row Trail		152.1	
	75.7	Johns Hollow Shelter	Sw	150.1	
	76.3	Va. 812 (USFS 36)	R	149.5	
	76.4	Rocky Row Run (760')	Cw	149.4	
	77.3	Lower Rocky Row Run bridge	w	148.5	
Va. Section 22	77.4	U.S. 501, Va. 130; **Big Island, Va., P.O. 24526; Glasgow, Va., P.O. 24555** (P.O.,G,M 5.6m E; P.O.,G,L,M 5.9m W; C,G 4.4m E)	RCGLM	148.4	
	77.6	James River Foot Bridge (678')		148.2	Va. Map 4
	78.8	Campsite	Cw	147.0	
	79.6	Matts Creek Shelter	Sw	146.2	
	81.5	Big Cove Branch	w	144.3	
	82.3	Sulphur Spring Trail (north crossing) (2,588')		143.5	
	82.8	Hickory Stand, Belfast Trail		143.0	
	84.6	Sulphur Spring Trail (south crossing)		141.2	
	85.1	Marble Spring	Cw	140.7	
	86.1	High Cock Knob (3,073')		139.7	

Natural Bridge A.T. Club

Central Virginia

	Miles from Rockfish Gap, Va.			Miles from New River, Va.	
Va. Section 23	87.3	Petites Gap, USFS 35; Blue Ridge Parkway, mile 71.0 (2,369')	R	138.5	
	88.7	Harrison Ground Spring	w	137.1	
	90.6	Thunder Ridge Overlook; Blue Ridge Parkway, mile 74.7 (3,501')	R	135.2	
	91.0	Lower Blue Ridge Parkway crossing, mile 74.9	R	134.8	
	92.0	Thunder Hill Shelter	Sw	133.8	
	92.3	Upper Blue Ridge Parkway crossing, mile 76.3	R	133.5	
	92.9	The Guillotine		132.9	
	93.2	Apple Orchard Mountain (4,225')		132.6	
Va. Section 24	94.6	Parkers Gap Road (USFS 812); Blue Ridge Parkway, mile 78.4 (3,430')	R	131.2	
	94.7	Apple Orchard Falls Trail		131.1	
	96.4	Black Rock		129.4	
	97.3	Cornelius Creek Shelter	Sw	128.5	
	97.9	Floyd Mountain (3,560')		127.9	
	102.3	Bryant Ridge Shelter (1,337')	Sw	123.5	
	104.4	Fork Mountain (2,042')		121.4	
Va. Section 25	106.0	Va. 614, Jennings Creek (951') (w 0.3m E; L,M 1.6m E, 4.5m W)	RLMw	119.8	
	107.5	Buchanan Trail		118.3	
	109.2	Cove Mountain Shelter	S(nw)	116.6	
	110.6	Little Cove Mountain Trail		115.2	
	111.0	Cove Mountain (2,720')		114.8	

Va. Map 4 — *Natural Bridge A.T. Club*

Central Virginia

GBS	N to S	Features	Facilities (see page 8 for codes)	S to N	Map
	Miles from Rockfish Gap, Va.			*Miles from New River, Va.*	
	112.4	Bearwallow Gap, Va. 43, Blue Ridge Parkway, mile 90.9 (2,228'); **Buchanan, Va., P.O. 24066** (P.O.,G,M 5m W; L 7m W; C,G,L,M 4.9m E)	RCGLM	113.4	
	114.2	Blue Ridge Parkway, mile 91.8; Mills Gap Overlook	R	111.6	
	114.9	Blue Ridge Parkway, mile 92.5; Sharp Top Overlook	R	110.9	
	115.6	Bobblets Gap Shelter (S,w 0.2m W)	Sw	110.2	
	118.0	Blue Ridge Parkway, mile 95.3; Harveys Knob Overlook	R	107.8	
	118.6	Blue Ridge Parkway, mile 95.9; Montvale Overlook	R	107.2	
	119.7	Blue Ridge Parkway, mile 97.0; Taylors Mountain Overlook	R	106.1	
	120.5	Black Horse Gap, Old Fincastle Road (USFS 186); Blue Ridge Parkway, mile 97.7 (2,402')	R	105.3	
	122.5	Spring	w	103.3	
	122.9	Wilson Creek Shelter	Sw	102.9	
	123.6	Wilson Creek	w	102.2	
	125.5	Curry Creek	w	100.3	
	126.3	Salt Pond Road (USFS 191)	R	99.5	
	128.7	Spring	w	97.1	
	129.1	Fullhardt Knob Shelter (2,676')	Sw	96.7	
	132.0	Va. 652	R	93.8	

Va. Section 26 — Natural Bridge A.T. Club
Va. Section 27 — Roanoke A.T. Club
Va. Map 4

Central Virginia

GBS	N to S	Features	Facilities (see page 8 for codes)		S to N	Map
	Miles from Rockfish Gap, Va.				*Miles from New River, Va.*	
	132.6	Norfolk & Western Railway, U.S. 11; **Troutville, Va., P.O. 24175** (P.O.,G 0.8m W)		RG	93.2	
	132.9	Va. 779, I-81		R	92.9	
	134.1	U.S. 220; **Daleville, Va., P.O. 24083; Cloverdale, Va., P.O. 24077** (P.O. 1m W; P.O.,G,L,M 2.3m E; G,L,M on A.T.)		RGLM	91.7	
	134.6	Tinker Creek (1,165')			91.2	
	138.1	Hay Rock, Tinker Ridge			87.7	
	139.2	Angels Gap			86.6	
	143.2	Lamberts Meadow Campsite, Sawmill Run		Cw	82.6	
	143.5	Lamberts Meadow Shelter		Sw	82.3	
	144.1	Scorched Earth Gap, Andy Layne Trail			81.7	
	144.6	Tinker Cliffs (3,000')			81.2	
	146.4	Brickey's Gap			79.4	
	149.5	Campbell Shelter		Sw	76.3	
	149.6	Pig Farm Campsite		Cw	76.2	
	150.2	McAfee Knob (3,197')			75.6	
	151.9	Catawba Mountain Shelter		Sw	73.9	
	152.9	Johns Spring Shelter		S	72.9	
	153.9	Va. 311; **Catawba, Va., P.O. 24070** (P.O.,G 1m W; L 1.7m W; M 1.3m W)		RGLM	71.9	
	158.2	Va. 785 (1,790') (L 0.9m E)		RL	67.6	

Va. Section 27 · Va. Section 28

Va. Map 4 · Roanoke A.T. Club

Central Virginia

	N to S	Features	Facilities (see page 8 for codes)	S to N	
	Miles from Rockfish Gap, Va.		*Miles from New River, Va.*		
	159.8	Va. 624, North Mountain Trail (G,L 0.4m W)	RGL	66.0	
	160.8	Rawies Rest		65.0	
	161.3	Lost Spectacles Gap		64.5	
	162.3	Dragons Tooth, Cove Mountain (3,020')		63.5	
	166.5	Pickle Branch Shelter (S,w 0.3m E)	Sw	59.3	
	167.5	Trout Creek, Va. 620 (1,525')	R	58.3	
	171.3	Audie Murphy Monument (3,100')		54.5	
	175.1	Craig Creek Valley, Va. 621 (1,540')	R	50.7	
	176.4	Niday Shelter	Sw	49.4	
	177.1	Cabin Branch	Cw	48.7	
	178.8	Sinking Creek Mountain (3,450')		47.0	
	182.4	Sarver Hollow Shelter (S,w 0.4m E)	Sw	43.4	
	185.5	Va. 630, Sinking Creek (2,100')	Rw	40.3	
	186.4	Sinking Creek Valley, Va. 42	R	39.4	
	187.8	Spring	w	38.0	
	188.8	Laurel Creek Shelter	Sw	37.0	
	191.8	Rocky Gap, Va. 601	R	34.0	
	192.8	Stream	w	33.0	
	193.8	Johns Creek Valley, USFS 156 (2,080')	Rw	32.0	
	194.6	War Spur Shelter	Sw	31.2	
	198.3	Campsites, spring	Cw	27.5	
	199.5	Wind Rock (4,100')		26.3	
	199.7	Salt Sulphur Turnpike (Va. 613)	R	26.1	
	203.4	Bailey Gap Shelter	S	22.4	
	203.6	Spring	w	22.2	
	204.9	Va. 635, Stony Creek (2,450')	R	20.9	
	205.9	Dismal Branch	w	19.9	

Left margin: Va. Section 29 · Va. Section 30 · Va. Section 31 · Va. Section 32 · Roanoke A.T. Club (RATC)

Right margin: Va. Map 3

Central Virginia

	Miles from Rockfish Gap, Va.			Miles from New River, Va.
	207.0	Va. 635, Stony Creek Valley	R	18.8
	207.3	Pine Swamp Branch Shelter	Sw	18.5
	209.8	Peters Mountain, Allegheny Trail (3,500')		16.0
	212.2	Dickinson Gap		13.6
	213.7	Groundhog Trail		12.1
	214.7	Symms Gap Meadow		11.1
	218.2	Campsite, water	Cw	7.6
	219.6	Rice Field Shelter (3,400') (S on A.T.; w 0.5m E)	Sw	6.2
	222.4	Springs	Cw	3.4
	224.6	Clendenin Road (Va. 641)	R	1.2
	225.8	U.S. 460, Senator Shumate Bridge (east end), New River (1,600') (G 0.1m E)	RG	0.0

Va. Section 33

Va. Map 3

RATC

Outdoor Club of Va. Tech (OCVT)

Southwest Virginia

GBS	N to S	Features	Facilities (see page 8 for codes)	S to N	Map
	Miles from New River, Va.			*Miles from Damascus, Va.*	
Roanoke A.T. Club; Va. Section 34	0.0	U.S. 460, Senator Shumate Bridge (east end), New River (1,600') (G 0.1m E)	RG	163.1	Va. Map 3
	0.5	Lane Street, **Pearisburg, Va., P.O. 24134** (P.O.,G,L,M 1m E; L 0.2m E)	RGLM	162.6	
	1.0	Va. 634	R	162.1	
	1.4	Spring	w	161.7	
	2.9	Angels Rest, Pearis Mountain (3,550')		160.2	
	3.4	Campsite, spring	Cw	159.7	
	8.7	Doc's Knob Shelter	Sw	154.4	
	10.9	Sugar Run Gap, Sugar Run Road (Va. 663)	R	152.2	
	12.5	Big Horse Gap, USFS 103 (3,800')	R	150.6	
	12.6	Ribble Trail, north junction	w	150.5	
	17.1	Wapiti Shelter (2,600')	Sw	146.0	
	18.6	Stream	w	144.5	
	19.0	Ribble Trail, south junction; White Pine Horse Campground (C,w 0.5m W)	Cw	144.1	
	22.9	Dismal Creek Falls Trail		140.2	
Va. 35	24.8	Va. 606 (2,100') (C,G,M,w 0.8m W)	RCGMw	138.3	
	24.9	Kimberling Creek		138.2	
	26.8	Brushy Mountain (2,900')		136.3	
Va. Section 36	30.1	Va. 608, Lickskillet Hollow (2,200') (G 0.8m E)	RG	133.0	Va. Map 2
	31.3	Jenny Knob Shelter	Sw	131.8	
	33.0	Brushy Mountain (3,101')		130.1	
	34.4	Va. 611	R	128.7	

Southwest Virginia

	N to S	Features	Facilities	S to N	
	Miles from New River, Va.			*Miles from Damascus, Va.*	
Va. Section 36	41.1	Helveys Mill Shelter (S,w 0.3m E)	Sw	122.0	OCVT
	42.6	Va. 612, Kimberling Creek	Rw	120.5	
	43.2	I-77 Crossing	R	119.9	
Va. Section 37	43.4	U.S. 21/52 (2,920'); **Bastian, Va., P.O. 24314; Bland, Va., P.O. 24315** (P.O. 1.8m W; P.O.,G,L,M 2.5m E)	RGLM	119.7	PATH
	50.3	Va. 615, Laurel Creek (2,450')	RC	112.8	
	50.7	Little Wolf Creek	w	112.4	
	53.5	Brushy Mountain (3,080')		109.6	
	54.9	Jenkins Shelter (2,470')	Sw	108.2	OCVT
	57.9	Davis Farm Campsite (C,w 0.5m W)	Cw	105.2	
Va. Section 38	58.7	Va. 623, Garden Mountain (3,900')	R	104.4	
	63.6	Walker Gap (3,520')	Rw	99.5	Va. Map 2
	64.9	Chestnut Knob Shelter (4,410')	S(nw)	98.2	Piedmont A.T. Hikers (PATH)
	66.7	Spring-fed pond	w	96.4	
	69.5	USFS 222 (2,300')	R	93.6	
	72.0	Lynn Camp Mountain (3,000')		91.1	
	73.5	Lynn Camp Creek (2,400')	w	89.6	
	73.8	Spring	w	89.3	
	73.9	Knot Maul Branch Shelter	S(nw)	89.2	
	75.2	Brushy Mountain (3,200')		87.9	
Va. Section 39	76.0	Va. 42; **Ceres, Va., P.O. 24318** (P.O. 5.2m E; w 0.2m E)	Rw	87.1	
	78.4	Va. 610	R	84.7	
	79.8	Tilson Gap, Big Walker Mountain (3,500')		83.3	
	81.5	Crawfish Valley (2,600') (w on A.T.; C,w 0.3m E)	Cw	81.6	

Southwest Virginia

GBS	N to S	Features	Facilities (see page 8 for codes)	S to N	Map
	Miles from New River, Va.			*Miles from Damascus, Va.*	
	82.6	Gullion (Little Brushy) Mountain (3,300')		80.5	
	85.1	Davis Path Shelter	S(nw)	78.0	
	86.0	Spring	w	77.1	
	86.7	Va. 617	R	76.4	
	87.8	Va. 683, U.S. 11, I-81 (2,420'); **Atkins, Va., P.O. 24311** (P.O.,G,M 3.2m W; G,L,M on A.T.)	RGLM	75.3	
	90.0	Va. 729	R	73.1	
	90.5	Va. 615	R	72.6	
	92.0	USFS 644	R	71.1	
	92.3	Chatfield Shelter	Sw	70.8	
	94.3	Glade Mountain (3,900')		68.8	
	95.2	USFS 86	RCw	67.9	
	95.6	Locust Mountain		67.5	
	98.1	Brushy Mountain		65.0	
	98.6	Va. 622	R	64.5	
	99.3	Va. 16 (3,220'); **Sugar Grove, Va., P.O. 24375** (P.O.,G,M 3.4m E; S,w on A.T; G 3m W)	RGMw	63.8	
	99.4	Partnership Shelter	Sw	63.7	
	103.4	Va. 601	R	59.7	
	107.2	Va. 670, South Fork Holston River (2,450')	R	55.9	
	108.5	Va. 672	R	54.6	
	110.0	Trimpi Shelter	Sw	53.1	
	111.8	High Point (3,700')		51.3	
	112.4	Raccoon Branch Campground (w 0.2m E; C,w 3.2m E)	Cw	50.7	
	113.9	Dickey Gap, Va. 16, Va. 650; **Troutdale, Va., P.O. 24378** (P.O.,G,M 2.6m E; L 3.8m E)	RGLM	49.2	

Va. Section 39
Va. Section 40
Va. Section 41
Va. Map 2
Va. Map 1

Mount Rogers A.T. Club | *Piedmont A.T. Hikers*

Southwest Virginia

	N to S	Features	Facilities	S to N	
	Miles from New River, Va.			*Miles from Damascus, Va.*	
Va. Section 42	115.1	Comers Creek (3,100')	w	48.0	Va. Map 1 — Mount Rogers A.T. Club
	116.0	Hurricane Campground Side Trail (C 0.5m W)	C	47.1	
	117.7	Stream	w	45.4	
	119.8	Stream	w	43.3	
	120.1	Chestnut Flats, Iron Mountain Trail		43.0	
	120.2	Hurricane Mountain Shelter	Sw	42.9	
	120.4	Hurricane Mountain (4,320')		42.7	
	122.4	Va. 603, Fox Creek (3,480') (C,w on A.T., 2m W)	RCw	40.7	
Va. Section 43	124.1	Old Orchard Shelter	Sw	39.0	
	125.8	Pine Mountain (4,960')		37.3	
	127.5	Stone Mountain		35.6	
	128.7	Spring	w	34.4	
	129.7	Campsites	Cw	33.4	
	130.0	Grayson Highlands State Park, Wise Shelter (4,460') (S,w on A.T.; C,w 2m E)	CSw	33.1	
	133.0	Wilburn Ridge		30.1	
	134.3	Rhododendron Gap (5,440')		28.8	
	135.1	Thomas Knob Shelter	Sw	28.0	
	135.5	Susan Spillane Trail to Mt. Rogers		27.6	
	137.3	Deep Gap	w	25.8	
Va. Section 44	139.3	Va. 600, Elk Garden (4,434') (G,M 3.5m W)	RGM	23.8	
	141.8	Whitetop Mountain Road (USFS 89)	RCw	21.3	
	142.0	Spring	w	21.1	
	142.5	Buzzard Rock, Whitetop Mountain (5,080')		20.6	
	145.0	Va. 601 (Beech Mountain Road)	Rw	18.1	

Southwest Virginia

	Miles from New River, Va.			Miles from Damascus, Va.	
	146.2	U.S. 58 (3,160'); Summit Cut, Va.	R	16.9	
	147.3	Lost Mountain Shelter	Sw	15.8	
	148.5	Va. 859 (Grassy Ridge Road)	R	14.6	
	149.1	Virginia Creeper Trail, Whitetop Laurel Creek		14.0	
	149.6	Va. 728, Creek Junction Station (2,700')	R	13.5	
	151.4	Campsite	C	11.7	
	152.6	Stream	w	10.5	
	153.7	Saunders Shelter (S,w 0.2m W)	Sw	9.4	
	154.0	Straight Mountain (3,500')		9.1	
	155.5	Taylors Valley Side Trail		7.6	
	156.2	Stream	w	6.9	
	157.5	U.S. 58, Straight Branch, Feathercamp Branch (2,250')	Rw	5.6	
	159.6	Feathercamp Ridge, Iron Mountain Trail (2,850')		3.5	
	162.1	U.S. 58, Virginia Creeper Trail	R	1.0	
	163.1	**Damascus, Va., P.O. 24236** (1,928') (P.O.,G,L,M on A.T.)	RGLM	0.0	

Va. Section 45

Mount Rogers A.T. Club

Va. Map 1

Tennessee–North Carolina

Miles from Damascus, Va. (N to S) — *Miles from Fontana Dam, N.C.* (S to N)

Tennessee Eastman Hiking Club

GBS	N to S	Features	Facilities (see page 8 for codes)	S to N	Map
Tenn.–N.C. Section 1	0.0	**Damascus, Va., P.O. 24236** (1,928') (P.O.,G,L,M on A.T.)	RGLM	296.2	Tenn.–N.C. Map 1
	1.9	Spring	w	294.3	
	3.5	Virginia–Tennessee Line		292.7	
	10.0	Abingdon Gap Shelter (3,785')	Sw	286.2	
	11.1	McQueens Gap, USFS 69	R	285.1	
	11.5	McQueens Knob		284.7	
	12.9	Double Spring Gap	w	283.3	
Tenn.–N.C. Section 2	14.8	Low Gap, U.S. 421 (3,384'); **Shady Valley, Tenn., P.O. 37688** (w on A.T.; P.O.,G,M 3m E)	RGMw	281.4	
	18.3	Double Springs Shelter, Holston Mountain Trail (4,080')	Sw	277.9	
	19.2	Campsite	w	277.0	
Tenn.–N.C. Section 3	21.3	Tenn. 91 (3,450')	R	274.9	
	24.6	Nick Grindstaff Monument		271.6	
	25.9	Iron Mountain Shelter (4,125')	S(nw)	270.3	
	26.1	Spring	w	270.1	
	27.5	Turkeypen Gap		268.7	
	28.9	Spring	w	267.3	
	32.7	Vandeventer Shelter (3,510') (S on A.T.; w 0.5m W)	Sw	263.5	
	34.4	Spring	w	261.8	
Tenn.–N.C. 4	37.1	Watauga Dam Road	R	259.1	
	38.4	Watauga Dam (north end)		257.8	
	39.5	Watauga Lake Shelter (2,100')	Sw	256.7	
	40.0	Griffith Branch	Cw	256.2	
	41.3	U.S. 321; **Hampton, Tenn., P.O. 37658** (P.O.,G,M 2.6m W; G,L 1.8m W)	RCGLM	254.9	

Tennessee–North Carolina

GBS	N to S	Features	Facilities (see page 8 for codes)	S to N	Map
		Miles from Damascus, Va.	*Miles from Fontana Dam, N.C.*		
	44.5	Pond Flats	Cw	251.7	
	47.5	Side trail to U.S. 321	w	248.7	
	48.3	Laurel Fork Shelter (2,400')	Sw	247.9	
	49.0	Laurel Fork Falls	w	247.2	
	50.2	Dennis Cove, USFS 50 (C,G,L,M 0.5m E; C,L 0.2m W)	RCGLMw	246.0	
	51.9	Trail to Coon Den Falls		244.3	
	54.9	White Rocks Mountain (4,206')		241.3	
	56.3	Moreland Gap Shelter	Sw	239.9	
	57.7	Campsite	Cw	238.5	
	61.6	Laurel Fork		234.6	
	62.6	Stream		233.6	
	63.8	Walnut Mountain Road	R	232.4	
	65.6	Campsite	Cw	230.6	
	67.8	Campsite	Cw	228.4	
	70.6	Campbell Hollow Road	R	225.6	
	70.9	Buck Mountain Road	R	225.3	
	73.8	Bear Branch Road	R	222.4	
	74.0	U.S. 19E (2,895'); **Roan Mountain, Tenn., P.O. 37687; Elk Park, N.C., P.O. 28622** (P.O.,G,M 3.4m W; P.O. 2.5m E; C 4.0m E; G 1.2m E; L 3m E; M 0.5m E, 1m E)	RCGLM	222.2	
	74.5	Apple House Shelter	S	221.7	
	74.6	Spring	w	221.6	
	77.0	Doll Flats	Cw	219.2	
	79.4	Hump Mountain (5,587')		216.8	
	80.3	Bradley Gap	Cw	215.9	
	81.1	Little Hump Mountain (5,459')	C	215.1	

GBS sidebar (top to bottom): Tenn.–N.C. 4 · Tennessee Eastman Hiking Club · Tenn.–N.C. Section 5 · Tenn.–N.C. Section 6

Map sidebar: Tenn.–N.C. Map 1 · Tenn.–N.C. Map 2

Tennessee–North Carolina

GBS	N to S	Features	Facilities (see page 8 for codes)	S to N	Map
	Miles from Damascus, Va.		*Miles from Fontana Dam, N.C.*		
Tenn.–N.C. 6	82.7	Yellow Mountain Gap, Overmountain Shelter (4,682') (C on A.T.; w 0.2m E; S 0.3m E)	CSw	213.5	
	84.4	Stan Murray Shelter (5,050')	Sw	211.8	
	85.8	Side trail to Grassy Ridge (C,w 0.5m E)	Cw	210.4	
Tenn.–N.C. 7	87.7	Carvers Gap, Tenn. 143, N.C. 261 (5,512')	Rw	208.5	
	89.2	Roan High Knob Shelter (6,285')	Sw	207.0	
	89.9	Side trail to Roan High Bluff	Rw	206.3	
	90.7	Ash Gap	Cw	205.5	
Tenn.–N.C. Section 8	92.5	Hughes Gap (4,040') (G 3.2m W; C,L 2m E)	RCGL	203.7	
	94.7	Little Rock Knob (4,918')		201.5	Tenn.–N.C. Map 2
	95.6	Clyde Smith Shelter	Sw	200.6	
	96.7	Campsite	Cw	199.5	
	97.5	Greasy Creek Gap (4,034') (C,w 0.2m W; L 0.7m E)	CLw	198.7	
	100.4	Stream	w	195.8	
	101.7	Iron Mountain Gap, Tenn. 107, N.C. 226 (3,723') (G 4.7m W)	RG	194.5	
Tenn.–N.C. Section 9	102.9	Little Bald Knob (4,459')		193.3	
	104.4	Cherry Gap Shelter	Sw	191.8	
	105.4	Low Gap (3,900')	w	190.8	
	107.1	Unaka Mountain (5,180')		189.1	
	108.1	USFS 230	R	188.1	
	108.7	Deep Gap (4,100')	Cw	187.5	
	109.7	Beauty Spot Gap	RCw	186.5	
	110.2	Beauty Spot		186.0	

Tennessee Eastman Hiking Club

Tennessee–North Carolina

GBS	N to S	Features	Facilities (see page 8 for codes)	S to N	Map
	Miles from Damascus, Va.		*Miles from Fontana Dam, N.C.*		
	111.4	USFS 230	R	184.8	Map 2
	112.5	Indian Grave Gap			
		(C 3.3m W)	RC	183.7	
	116.6	Curley Maple Gap Shelter (3,070')	Sw	179.6	
	119.5	Nolichucky River Valley			
		(C,L,M on A.T.)	RCLM	176.7	
	120.8	Nolichucky River (1,700'); **Erwin, Tenn., P.O. 37650**			
		(P.O.,G,M 3.8m W; L 1.2m W; G,L 2.3m W)	RGLM	175.4	
	124.7	Temple Hill Gap (2,850')		171.5	
	127.1	No Business Knob Shelter	S	169.1	
	127.3	Spring	w	168.9	
	131.4	Ogelsby Branch	w	164.8	Map 3
	132.0	Spivey Gap, U.S. 19W (3,200')			
		(C,w 0.5m W)	RCw	164.2	
	132.5	Campsite	Cw	163.7	
	134.0	Trail to High Rocks (4,100')		162.2	Tenn.–N.C. Map 3
	134.3	Whistling Gap	Cw	161.9	
	136.3	Little Bald		159.9	
	137.3	Campsite	Cw	158.9	
	137.7	Bald Mountain Shelter	Sw	158.5	
	138.6	Big Stamp			
		(C,w 0.3m W; M 1.5m E)	CMw	157.6	
	138.8	Big Bald (5,516')		157.4	
	139.6	Spring	w	156.6	
	141.6	Low Gap	Cw	154.6	
	143.0	Street Gap (4,100')		153.2	
	144.6	Springs	w	151.6	

(Left margin vertical labels: Carolina Mountain Club; Tennessee Eastman Hiking Club; Tenn.–N.C. 9; Tenn.–N.C. Section 10; Tenn.–N.C. Section 11)

Tennessee–North Carolina

GBS	N to S	Features	Facilities (see page 8 for codes)	S to N	Map
	Miles from Damascus, Va.		*Miles from Fontana Dam, N.C.*		
	145.3	Sams Gap, U.S. 23, I-26 (3,800') (M 1.9m E, 2.8m E; G 3.2m E)	RGM	150.9	
	147.1	High Rock (4,460')		149.1	
	147.7	Hogback Ridge Shelter (S 0.1m E; w 0.3m E)	Sw	148.5	
	148.9	Rice Gap (3,800')	R	147.3	
	149.9	Big Flat	Cw	146.3	
	150.5	Frozen Knob (4,579')		145.7	
	153.3	Rector Laurel Road (2,960')	R	142.9	
	153.8	Devil Fork Gap, N.C. 212	R	142.4	
	155.6	Campsite	Cw	140.6	
	156.5	Flint Mountain Shelter (3,550')	Sw	139.7	
	159.2	Spring	w	137.0	
	160.5	Big Butt (4,750')	C	135.7	
	162.4	Jerry Cabin Shelter (4,150')	Sw	133.8	
	164.9	Big Firescald Knob	w	131.3	
	165.9	Blackstack Cliffs		130.3	
	166.2	Spring	w	130.0	
	167.9	Camp Creek Bald, side trail to fire tower (4,750')	R	128.3	
	169.2	Little Laurel Shelter (3,300')	Sw	127.0	
	172.5	Log Cabin Drive	R	123.7	
	174.1	Allen Gap, N.C. 208, Tenn. 70 (2,234')	Rw	122.1	
	176.3	Spring	w	119.9	
	177.8	Spring Mountain Shelter (3,300')	Sw	118.4	
	179.5	Hurricane Gap	R	116.7	
	180.6	Rich Mountain Fire Tower Side Trail (3,600')	Cw	115.6	
	182.9	Tanyard Gap, U.S. 25 & 70 (2,278')	R	113.3	
	183.9	Campsite	Cw	112.3	

Left margin: Tenn.–N.C. Section 12 · Tenn.–N.C. Section 13 · Tenn.–N.C. Section 14

Right margin: Tenn.–N.C. Map 3 · Tenn.–N.C. Map 4 · Carolina Mountain Club

Tennessee–North Carolina

GBS	N to S	Features	Facilities (see page 8 for codes)	S to N	Map
	Miles from Damascus, Va.			*Miles from Fontana Dam, N.C.*	
14	185.5	Pump Gap		110.7	Tenn.–N.C. Map 4
	187.4	Lovers Leap Rock		108.8	
	188.8	U.S. 25 & 70, N.C. 209 (1,326'); **Hot Springs, N.C., P.O. 28743** (P.O.,C,G,L,M on A.T.)	RCGLM	107.4	
Tenn.–N.C. Section 15	192.0	Deer Park Mountain Shelter	Sw	104.2	
	195.4	Garenflo Gap (2,500')	R	100.8	
	197.9	Big Rock Spring	w	98.3	
	199.5	Bluff Mountain (4,686')		96.7	
	201.9	Walnut Mountain Shelter	Sw	94.3	
	203.2	Lemon Gap, N.C. 1182, Tenn. 107 (3,550')	R	93.0	
	206.8	Roaring Fork Shelter	Sw	89.4	
	208.6	Max Patch Summit (4,629')		87.6	
	209.4	Max Patch Road (N.C. 1182)	R	86.8	
	212.1	Brown Gap	RCw	84.1	
	215.0	Deep Gap, Groundhog Creek Shelter (2,900') (S,w 0.2m E)	Sw	81.2	
Tenn.–N.C. Section 16	217.0	Campsite	Cw	79.2	
	217.5	Snowbird Mountain (4,263')	R	78.7	
	219.0	Spanish Oak Gap		77.2	
	219.9	Painter Branch	Cw	76.3	
	222.2	Waterville School Road (C,G,L 0.2m W)	RCGL	74.0	
	222.7	I-40	R	73.5	
	223.1	Pigeon River (1,400')		73.1	
	223.3	State Line Branch	Cw	72.9	

Carolina Mountain Club

Tennessee–North Carolina

GBS	N to S	Features	Facilities (see page 8 for codes)	S to N	Map

Miles from Damascus, Va.

Miles from Fontana Dam, N.C.

	N to S	Features	Facilities	S to N	
	224.6	Davenport Gap, Tenn. 32, N.C. 284; eastern boundary, Great Smoky Mountains National Park (1,975') (G,L,M 1.3m E; C 2.5m E)	RCGLM	71.6	
	225.5	Davenport Gap Shelter	Sw	70.7	
	227.7	Spring	w	68.5	
	229.3	Spring	w	66.9	
	229.8	Mt. Cammerer Side Trail (5,000')		66.4	
	232.6	Cosby Knob Shelter	Sw	63.6	
	233.2	Cosby Knob		63.0	
	236.5	Snake Den Ridge Trail		59.7	
	238.4	Mt. Guyot Side Trail		57.8	
	238.5	Guyot Spring	w	57.7	
	239.1	Guyot Spur (6,360')		57.1	
	240.3	Tri-Corner Knob Shelter	Sw	55.9	
	241.3	Mt. Chapman		54.9	
	242.8	Mt. Sequoyah		53.4	
	245.5	Pecks Corner Shelter (w on A.T.; S,w 0.5m E)	Sw	50.7	
	246.8	Bradleys View		49.4	
	250.1	Porters Gap, the Sawteeth		46.1	
	252.0	Charlies Bunion		44.2	
	252.9	Icewater Spring Shelter	Sw	43.3	
	253.2	Boulevard Trail to Mt. LeConte		43.0	
	255.9	Newfound Gap, U.S. 441 (5,045')	Rw	40.3	
	257.6	Indian Gap	R	38.6	
	260.4	Mt. Collins Shelter (5,900') (S,w 0.5m W)	Sw	35.8	
	262.6	Mt. Love		33.6	

Left margin: Tenn.–N.C. Section 17 (N.C. 1) | 18 (N.C. 2)

Right margin: Smoky Mountains Hiking Club | Great Smoky Mtns. N.P. Map

Tennessee–North Carolina

GBS	N to S	Features	Facilities (see page 8 for codes)	S to N	Map
	Miles from Damascus, Va.			*Miles from Fontana Dam, N.C.*	
	263.8	Clingmans Dome (6,643') (R,w 0.5m E)	Rw	32.4	
	266.7	Double Spring Gap Shelter (5,507')	Sw	29.5	
	268.2	Silers Bald		28.0	
	268.4	Silers Bald Shelter	Sw	27.8	
	271.1	Buckeye Gap (4,817')	w	25.1	
	273.7	Sams Gap	w	22.5	
	273.9	Derrick Knob Shelter	Sw	22.3	
	275.0	Sugar Tree Gap (4,435')		21.2	
	277.4	Mineral Gap (5,030')		18.8	
	278.1	Beechnut Gap	w	18.1	
	278.4	Thunderhead, east peak (5,527')		17.8	
	279.0	Rocky Top		17.2	
	280.2	Eagle Creek Trail to Spence Field Shelter, Bote Mountain Trail (S,w 0.2m E)	Sw	16.0	
	283.1	Russell Field Shelter	Sw	13.1	
	283.9	Little Abrams Gap (4,120')		12.3	
	285.3	Devils Tater Patch (4,775')		10.9	
	285.6	Mollies Ridge Shelter	Sw	10.6	
	287.3	Ekaneetlee Gap (3,842')	w	8.9	
	288.7	Doe Knob (4,520')		7.5	
	291.0	Birch Spring Gap	Cw	5.2	
	292.2	Shuckstack		4.0	
	296.2	Little Tennessee River, Fontana Dam; southern boundary, Great Smoky Mountains National Park (1,800')	R	0.0	

Smoky Mountains Hiking Club

Tenn.–N.C. Section 18 (N.C. 2)

Great Smoky Mtns. N.P. Map

GBS	N to S	Features	Facilities (see page 8 for codes)	S to N	Map

Miles from Fontana Dam, N.C.   *Miles from Springer Mountain, Ga.*

	N to S	Features	Facilities	S to N	
N.C. Section 3	0.0	Little Tennessee River, Fontana Dam; southern boundary, Great Smoky Mountains National Park (1,800')	R	163.3	ATC Nantahala N.F. Map
	0.4	Fontana Dam Visitor Center	Rw	162.9	
	0.7	Fontana Dam Shelter	Sw	162.6	
	1.8	N.C. 28; **Fontana Dam, N.C., P.O. 28733** (P.O.,G,L,M 2m W)	RGLM	161.5	
	4.3	Campsite	Cw	159.0	
	4.5	Walker Gap (3,450')		158.8	
	5.9	Black Gum Gap		157.4	
	7.3	Cable Gap Shelter	Sw	156.0	
N.C. Section 4	8.2	Yellow Creek Gap, Yellow Creek Mountain Road (2,980') (L 4m E)	RL	155.1	
	10.6	Cody Gap	Cw	152.7	
	11.4	Hogback Gap		151.9	
	13.2	Brown Fork Gap	w	150.1	
	13.4	Brown Fork Gap Shelter	Sw	149.9	
	14.8	Sweetwater Gap		148.5	
N.C. Section 5	15.8	Stecoah Gap, N.C. 143 (3,165') (Sweetwater Creek Road)	Rw	147.5	Smoky Mountains Hiking Club
	17.9	Simp Gap		145.4	
	18.9	Locust Cove Gap	Cw	144.4	
	21.3	Cheoah Bald (5,062')		142.0	
	22.5	Sassafras Gap Shelter	Sw	140.8	
	23.4	Swim Bald		139.9	
	26.3	Grassy Gap (3,050')		137.0	
	27.8	Wright Gap	R	135.5	

North Carolina–Georgia

GBS	N to S Miles from Fontana Dam, N.C.	Features	Facilities (see page 8 for codes)	S to N Miles from Springer Mountain, Ga.	Map
N.C. Section 6	29.4	U.S. 19, U.S. 74, Nantahala River (1,740'); Wesser, N.C. (L,M on A.T.; G 1m E)	RGLM	133.9	ATC Nantahala N.F. Map
	30.2	A. Rufus Morgan Shelter	Sw	133.1	
	33.5	Jump-up Lookout (4,000')		129.8	
	35.1	Wesser Creek Trail, Wesser Bald Shelter	CS	128.2	
	35.2	Spring	w	128.1	
	35.9	Wesser Bald (4,627')		127.4	
N.C. Section 7	37.3	Tellico Gap, N.C. 1365 (3,850')	R	126.0	
	38.7	Spring	w	124.6	
	39.0	Side trail to Rocky Bald Lookout		124.3	
	40.2	Copper Ridge Bald Lookout (5,080')		123.1	
	40.9	Cold Spring Shelter	CSw	122.4	
	42.1	Burningtown Gap, N.C. 1397 (4,236')	R	121.2	
	44.4	Licklog Gap (w 0.5m W)	w	118.9	
	46.2	Campsite	Cw	117.1	
	46.6	Wayah Bald (5,342')	R	116.7	
	48.5	Wine Spring	Cw	114.8	
	49.0	USFS 69	Rw	114.3	
N.C. Section 8	50.8	Wayah Gap, N.C. 1310 (4,130')	R	112.5	
	53.0	Siler Bald Shelter (4,700') (S,w 0.5m E)	Sw	110.3	
	54.7	Panther Gap		108.6	
	55.6	Swinging Lick Gap		107.7	
	55.8	Campsite	Cw	107.5	
	56.7	Winding Stair Gap, U.S. 64; **Franklin, N.C., P.O. 28734** (w on A.T.; P.O.,G,L,M 10m E)	RGLMw	106.6	

North Carolina–Georgia

GBS	N to S	Features	Facilities (see page 8 for codes)	S to N	Map
	Miles from Fontana Dam, N.C.			*Miles from Springer Mountain, Ga.*	
	59.8	Wallace Gap, Old U.S. 64 (3,738')	R	103.5	
	60.4	Rock Gap, Standing Indian Campground (C 1.5m W)	RC	102.9	
	60.5	Rock Gap Shelter	Sw	102.8	
	63.0	Glassmine Gap		100.3	
	65.8	Big Spring Shelter	Sw	97.5	
	66.4	Albert Mountain (5,250')		96.9	
	66.7	Bear Pen Trail, USFS 67	R	96.6	
	67.8	Spring	w	95.5	
	68.0	Mooney Gap, USFS 83	R	95.3	
	68.9	Betty Creek Gap (4,300')	Cw	94.4	
	72.6	Carter Gap Shelter	Sw	90.7	
	73.0	Timber Ridge Trail		90.3	
	75.8	Beech Gap (4,460')	Cw	87.5	
	78.7	Lower Trail Ridge Trail, Standing Indian Mountain (5,498') (w 0.2m W)	w	84.6	
	80.2	Standing Indian Shelter	Sw	83.1	
	81.1	Deep Gap, USFS 71 (4,341')	Rw	82.2	
	83.2	Wateroak Gap		80.1	
	84.1	Chunky Gal Trail		79.2	
	84.4	Whiteoak Stamp		78.9	
	85.1	Muskrat Creek Shelter (4,600')	Sw	78.2	
	86.0	Sassafras Gap		77.3	

N.C. Section 9

N.C. Section 10

ATC Nantahala N.F. Map

Nantahala Hiking Club

North Carolina–Georgia

Miles from
Fontana Dam, N.C.

Miles from
Springer Mountain, Ga.

	N to S	Features	Facilities	S to N	
	87.9	Bly Gap (3,840')	Cw	75.4	
	88.1	North Carolina–Georgia Line		75.2	
	89.9	Rich Cove Gap		73.4	
	90.1	Campsite	Cw	73.2	
	91.1	Blue Ridge Gap (3,020')		72.2	
	91.7	As Knob		71.6	
	92.4	Plumorchard Gap Shelter (S,w 0.2m E)	Sw	70.9	
	93.5	Bull Gap		69.8	
	94.9	Cowart Gap		68.4	
	95.6	Campsite	Cw	67.7	
	96.7	Dicks Creek Gap, U.S. 76 (2,675'); **Hiawassee, Ga., P.O. 30546** (w on A.T.; L 3.5m W; P.O.,G,L,M 11m W)	RGLMw	66.6	
	97.2	Streams	w	66.1	
	97.9	Moreland Gap		65.4	
	98.9	Powell Mountain (3,850')		64.4	
	99.1	McClure Gap	C	64.2	
	100.2	Deep Gap Shelter (3,550') (S,w 0.3m E)	Sw	63.1	
	100.9	Kelly Knob (4,276')		62.4	
	102.0	Addis Gap (3,304') (w 0.5m E)	Cw	61.3	
	102.8	Sassafras Gap	w	60.5	
	103.9	Blue Ridge Swag		59.4	
	107.3	Tray Mountain Shelter (S 0.2m W; w 0.3m W)	Sw	56.0	
	107.6	Tray Mountain (4,430')		55.7	
	108.4	Tray Gap, Tray Mountain Road (USFS 79)	R	54.9	

Left margin (top to bottom): Georgia A.T. Club · N.C. Section 11 · Ga. Section 12

Right margin: ATC Chattahoochee N.F. Map

North Carolina–Georgia

GBS	N to S	Features	Facilities (see page 8 for codes)	S to N	Map

Miles from Fontana Dam, N.C.

Miles from Springer Mountain, Ga.

	N to S	Features	Facilities	S to N	
Ga. Section 12	109.2	Cheese Factory Site	Cw	54.1	ATC Chattahoochee N.F. Map — Georgia A.T. Club
	109.4	Tray Mountain Road (USFS 79)	R	53.9	
	110.1	Indian Grave Gap (3,113')	R	53.2	
	111.5	Rocky Mountain (4,017')	C	51.8	
	112.2	Stream	w	51.1	
	112.8	Unicoi Gap, Ga. 75 (2,949'); **Helen, Ga., P.O. 30545** (P.O.,G,L,M 9m E; C,G,L,M 3.8m W)	RCGLM	50.5	
Ga. Section 13	114.2	Blue Mountain (4,025')		49.1	
	115.0	Blue Mountain Shelter	Sw	48.3	
	115.7	Spring	w	47.6	
	115.9	Campsite	C	47.4	
	116.6	Red Clay Gap		46.7	
	117.2	Chattahoochee Gap (3,500')	w	46.1	
	118.4	Cold Springs Gap		44.9	
	120.8	Poplar Stamp Gap	Cw	42.5	
	122.2	Low Gap Shelter (3,050')	Sw	41.1	
	122.8	Sheep Rock Top		40.5	
	124.5	Poor Mountain		38.8	
	125.5	White Oak Stamp		37.8	
	126.4	Hog Pen Gap, Ga. 348 (3,450')	Rw	36.9	
	126.6	Whitley Gap Shelter (S 1.2m E; w 1.5m E)	Sw	36.7	
Ga. Section 14	127.3	Tesnatee Gap, Ga. 348 (3,138')	R	36.0	
	128.1	Cowrock Mountain (3,842')		35.2	
	128.6	Baggs Creek Gap	Cw	34.7	
	129.4	Wolf Laurel Top		33.9	
	129.5	Corbin Horse Stamp		33.8	
	130.0	Rock Spring Top	w	33.3	
	130.7	Swaim Gap		32.6	

North Carolina–Georgia

Miles from Fontana Dam, N.C. — *Miles from Springer Mountain, Ga.*

Georgia A.T. Club

GBS	N to S	Features	Facilities (see page 8 for codes)	S to N	Map
Ga. 14	131.3	Levelland Mountain (3,942')		32.0	ATC Chattahoochee N.F. Map
	131.7	Bull Gap	Cw	31.6	
Ga. Section 15	132.8	Neels Gap, U.S. 19/129 (3,125') (G,L on A.T.; L 0.3m E; C,G 3m W; C,L 3.5m W)	RCGLw	30.5	
	133.8	Flatrock Gap, Trail to Byron Reece Memorial (w 0.2m W)	w	29.5	
	135.2	Blood Mountain Shelter (4,461')	S(nw)	28.1	
	136.0	Slaughter Creek Campsite	Cw	27.3	
	136.1	Stream	w	27.2	
	136.4	Bird Gap (3,650')	C	26.9	
	136.5	Woods Hole Shelter (S,w 0.4m W)	Sw	26.8	
	137.8	Jarrard Gap (3,250') (w 0.3m W; w 1m W, G,L 2m W)	GLw	25.5	
	138.3	Burnett Field Mountain		25.0	
	141.1	Dan Gap		22.2	
	142.4	Big Cedar Mountain (3,737')		20.9	
Ga. Section 16	143.4	Woody Gap, Ga. 60 (3,150'); **Suches, Ga., P.O. 30572** (w 0.1m W; P.O.,G 2m W)	RGw	19.9	
	144.8	Ramrock Mountain		18.5	
	147.0	Gooch Gap, USFS 42 (2,784')	Rw	16.3	
	148.4	Gooch Mountain Shelter	CSw	14.9	
	149.7	Justus Creek (2,550')	Cw	13.6	
	151.1	Justus Mountain (3,224')		12.2	
	151.7	Cooper Gap, USFS 42/80	R	11.6	
	153.3	Horse Gap (2,673')	R	10.0	
	155.2	Hightower Gap, USFS 42/69	R	8.1	

North Carolina–Georgia

Miles from Fontana Dam, N.C.

Miles from Springer Mountain, Ga.

N to S	Features	Facilities	S to N
155.7	Hawk Mountain Shelter (S 0.2m W; w 0.4m W)	Sw	7.6
157.5	Logging Road	R	5.8
158.4	Side trail to Long Creek Falls		4.9
159.2	Three Forks, USFS 58 (2,530')	RCw	4.1
159.7	Stover Creek	w	3.6
160.8	Stover Creek Shelter	Sw	2.5
162.4	USFS 42	R	0.9
163.1	Springer Mountain Shelter (C,S,w 0.2m E)	CSw	0.2
163.3	Springer Mountain (3,782')		0.0

Ga. Section 17

ATC Chattahoochee N.F. Map

Georgia A.T. Club

Amicalola Falls Approach Trail

GBS	N to S	Features	Facilities (see page 8 for codes)	S to N	Map
	Miles from Springer Mountain, Ga.		*Miles from Amicalola Falls State Park*		
	0.0	Springer Mountain (3,782')		8.8	
	1.5	Black Gap Shelter	CSw	7.3	
	2.8	Nimblewill Gap, USFS 28 (3,100')	R	6.0	
	3.4	Side trail to Len Foote Hike Inn (L,M,w 1m E)	LMw	5.4	
	3.7	Frosty Mountain Road (USFS 46)	R	5.1	
	4.0	Frosty Mountain (3,382')	Cw	4.8	
	5.6	High Shoals Road	R	3.2	
	7.4	Side trail to Len Foote Hike Inn (L,M,w 5m E)	LMw	1.4	
	7.6	Amicalola Lodge Road (L,M,w 0.2m E)	RLMw	1.2	
	8.8	Visitors Center, Amicalola Falls State Park (1,700')	RCSw	0.0	

Georgia A.T. Club — Approach Trail

ATC Chattahoochee N.F. Map

A.T. Maintaining Clubs

Maine A.T. Club	www.matc.org
Appalachian Mountain Club	www.outdoors.org
Dartmouth Outing Club	www.dartmouth.edu/~doc
Green Mountain Club	www.greenmountainclub.org
AMC Berkshire Chapter	www.amcberkshire.org
AMC Connecticut Chapter	www.ct-amc.org
New York–New Jersey Trail Conference	www.nynjtc.org
Wilmington Trail Club	www.wilmingtontrailclub.org
Batona Hiking Club	members.aol.com/Batona
AMC Delaware Valley Chapter	www.amcdv.org
Philadelphia Trail Club	m.zanger.tripod.com
Blue Mountain Eagle Climbing Club	www.bmecc.org
Allentown Hiking Club	www.allentownhikingclub.org
Susquehanna A.T. Club	www.satc-hike.org
York Hiking Club	www.yorkhikingclub.com
Cumberland Valley A.T. Club	geocities.com/cvatclub
Mountain Club of Maryland	www.mcomd.org
Potomac A.T. Club	www.patc.net
Old Dominion A.T. Club	www.odatc.org
Tidewater A.T. Club	www.tidewateratc.org
Natural Bridge A.T. Club	www.nbatc.org
Roanoke A.T. Club	www.ratc.org
Outdoor Club of Virginia Tech	www.outdoor.org.vt.edu
Piedmont A.T. Hikers	www.path-at.org
Mount Rogers A.T. Club	www.geocities.com/Yosemite/Geyser/2539
Tennessee Eastman Hiking Club	www.tehcc.org
Carolina Mountain Club	www.carolinamtnclub.com
Smoky Mountains Hiking Club	www.smhclub.org
Nantahala Hiking Club	www.maconweb.com/nhc
Georgia A.T. Club	www.georgia-atclub.org

History of the *Appalachian Trail Data Book*

The model for the *Appalachian Trail Data Book* was the Mileage Fact Sheet compiled by Ed Garvey and Gus Crews, published simultaneously in 1971 by the Appalachian Trail Conference and Appalachian Books (Oakton, Va.) as an appendix to Mr. Garvey's *Appalachian Hiker.*

The first edition (1977) of the *Appalachian Trail Data Book* was compiled by Raymond F. Hunt of Kingsport, Tenn., who continued to perform this volunteer service annually until 1983, when he began a six-year term as chair of the Appalachian Trail Conference.

The 1984 and subsequent editions have been compiled by another volunteer, Daniel D. Chazin of Teaneck, N.J., an officer of the New York–New Jersey Trail Conference and editor of the *Appalachian Trail Guide to New York–New Jersey.* Mr. Chazin draws each fall on the work of field editors of the other 10 guidebooks and more than 30 other volunteer data compilers and Conservancy representatives for information on the various sections of the Appalachian Trail.

Incident Reporting Form—2006

(Please see page 3 for reporting emergencies.)

Name: _____ Today's date: _____

Daytime phone: _____ Evening phone: _____

Mailing address: _____

_____

Type of Incident

☐ Crime
  (type: _____)

☐ Fire

☐ Search/rescue/
  medical emergency

☐ Theft/personal property

☐ Disorderly behavior

☐ Drug/alcohol abuse

☐ Vandalism

☐ Other (_____)

☐ Trespass

☐ Resource damage

☐ Dumping

☐ ATV/ORV use

Date/time of incident: _____

Location (please be as specific as possible: *Data Book* page, location, mileage, etc.) _____

_____

Who was involved? _____

_____

Witnesses: _____

_____

What happened? _____

_____

_____

_____

_____

_____

_____

Were law-enforcement, fire, search/rescue personnel involved/contacted? ☐Y ☐N

If so, which agency? _____

Name of contact there: _____

Telephone: _____

**Please tear out this page, fold the completed form in half, and mail it to
ATC at the address on the other side (no postage necessary).**

BUSINESS REPLY MAIL
FIRST CLASS   PERMIT NO. 6   HARPERS FERRY, W.VA.

POSTAGE WILL BE PAID BY ADDRESSEE

APPALACHIAN TRAIL CONSERVANCY
P.O. Box 807
799 Washington Street
Harpers Ferry, WV 25425-9988